MW00629306

Ocracoke Lighthouse and The Old Salts

By Ellen Fulcher Cloud

*Ocracoke Lighthouse**

*Old Salt**

Portsmouth: The Way It Was

*included in this volume

Ocracoke Lighthouse and The Old Salts

25TH ANNIVERSARY
OMNIBUS EDITION

Ellen Fulcher Cloud

 For information, address Beach Glass Books, P.O. Box 72672, North Chesterfield, VA 23235.

Omnibus Edition Published by Beach Glass Books, 2018
Manufactured in the United States of America
First Printing 2018

Front cover photograph by rpernell/iStock
Back cover photograph by M.V. Watson,
courtesy National Park Service
Author photograph from the author's collection
Book design by Ray McAllister

Ellen Fulcher Cloud, 1940-2016
Ocracoke Lighthouse and The Old Salts / by Ellen Fulcher Cloud
ISBN 978-0-9987881-3-5

To Sally Newell &
Kevin Cutler,
for their help in saving the windows
of Ocracoke Lighthouse

&

To the Memory of an Old Salt,
my father,
Captain Elmo Fulcher

Contents

CONTENTS (cont.)

Foreword

FOR THE 25TH ANNIVERSARY
OMINBUS EDITION

The reissuing of Ellen Fulcher Cloud's *Portsmouth: The Way It Was* in 2017 might have been a one and done. That project was a natural, suggested by a bookstore owner whose customers often ask about the "ghost village of the Outer Banks." Ellen herself was enthusiastic and resecured her publishing rights. Sadly, however, she then passed away. We published *Portsmouth* with the help of her daughters, Deidra Cloud Ramsey and Simona Rae Spickett. The book was as well received as we expected.

It seemed practical to bring out another.

But what? True, Ellen's dogged research—conducted before the age of the Internet, mind you—had resulted in a three-book "Island History." *Portsmouth* was the third book, leaving her first two as prospects. *Ocracoke Lighthouse* was fewer than a hundred pages, however, while *Old Salt* was barely more. Indeed, Ellen referred to each as a "booklet."

The solution, then, was ... both. Ellen had worked on the two Ocracoke books at the same time. Indeed, she wrote the preface for the second in December 1992—actually three months *before* writing the preface to the *first* book.

The books carry a similar voice and a similar feel, and even a similar format: an opening overview, several chapters of historical findings, and then an entertaining first-person chapter to close. They mesh well.

The problem was materials. There were no available design files or photographs, as there had been for *Portsmouth*. My wife Vicki and her sister, Lori Pettis, were able to extract the text for use. (Vicki later aided in proofreading, as well.) Finding photographs was tougher. Fortunately, Pam Davis Morris of the Core Sound Waterfowl Museum and Heritage Center produced high-quality scans of eight photos that Deidra found in museum files—and of a photo of Deidra's grandfather that she realized she had hanging on her wall at home! The Ocracoke Preservation Society helped with more. Others were found online. The rest we scanned from the original books and enhanced them as best we could. If some look old, well, keep in mind that they *are* old.

Ellen's words have stood the test of time, needing only a very few notes for updating and some minor shuffling. One chapter, a list of lighthouse keepers at other locations, was removed to the appendix. Two chapters listing boat pilots and boats were combined with chapters on those subjects. And chapters on three separate wars were combined into one, exactly as Ellen had done with *Portsmouth*. We even included two pieces of extra material that Ellen wrote after the books were published.

The omnibus edition that has emerged, just in time for the 25th anniversary of *Ocracoke Lighthouse*, is a worthy companion to *Portsmouth*. Through Beach Glass Books, we have been able to add more pages, more images, modern photo reproduction, and a hardcover binding. *Ocracoke Lighthouse and The Old Salts* offers a thorough look at both the lighthouse and at Ocracoke's seafaring history, possibly the most important works on the two most important aspects of island life. No Outer Banks library should be without it.

Ellen's passion fills this edition. One can't help but be caught up in the island's story. Even the daily logs of a lighthouse keeper, for instance, transport the reader to a different time on this distant island:

> ***1913: JULY 10th.*** *The four masted schooner* V. Josephine *of Baltimore Md. went ashore at Ocracoke Inlet on the morning of July 10th 1913 at 4 am. Assistance was rendered by Ocracoke and Portsmouth Lifesaving Stations. Cause of Casualty—Ocracoke Light was mistaken for Bodie Island Light. ...* ***SEPT. 3rd.*** *Hurrican[e] on the night of the 2nd and morning of 3rd. From NE to SE blew and washed down part of the fence, plank walks, slightly damaged by sea tide and did very much damage to trees inside reservation....*

You'll also surely enjoy Ellen's own story of "The Great Window Heist" ("Realizing as we drove off, the seriousness of removing federal property without permission...") and her touching tribute to one particular "Old Salt" ("He was a man of dry humor with a sparkle in his eye... He was a plain, hard-working, down-to-earth man, my father.").

But mostly you'll appreciate Ocracoke's story. As Ellen explains:

"I feel it is imperative that this history be remembered, that something needs to be done to acknowledge this rich heritage of our forefathers. ... This booklet is an attempt to remind Ocracokers of who we are, to remind us of what we want to be, to help us put our priorities in order and to stop and look at where we are going."

No one has said it better.

RAY McALLISTER
Richmond, Virginia
February 2018

PART I

OCRACOKE LIGHTHOUSE

Ocracoke Lighthouse, 1993, original cover
(Photograph by Paulette Chitwood)

AUTHOR COLLECTION, DIGITAL PRINT COURTESY OF CORE SOUND WATERFOWL MUSEUM AND HERITAGE CENTER

PREFACE

March 1993

I was born and reared on Ocracoke Island, and, like most other Ocracokers, have thought little about the history of Ocracoke Lighthouse. It was a part of everyday life here and gave us a feeling of security that we were not even aware of until one night when it ceased to operate.

Because of this, and because of the one question asked thousands of times by visitors to the Island—"Where can I find the history of the lighthouse?"—I have put together here a brief history.

Ocracoke Lighthouse is the oldest on the Outer Banks and the shortest. It is the second oldest still in operation on the East coast of the United States. The tower is sixty-five feet high, with an overall height of seventy-five feet including the lantern. The tower is built of brick with hand-spread mortar covering the exterior walls. The walls at the base of the tower are five feet thick. The eight-thousand-candle-power fixed white electric light invisible for fourteen miles. It was built in 1823 to replace a lighthouse on Shell Castle Island that became useless because of shifting channels and sand bars. The present lighthouse and a three-room keeper's quarters were constructed in 1823. The keeper's quarters have been expanded twice to make two living quarters, which are now occupied by rangers of the Cape Hatteras National Park. The lighthouse itself is essentially unchanged except for updating of equipment. Thousands of visitors visit the site each year. It is one of the most picturesque spots on the island.

ELLEN FULCHER CLOUD

Ocracoke Lighthouse in the 1950s, photographed by Aycock Brown

OUTER BANKS HISTORY CENTER, MANTEO, N.C.
THE AYCOCK BROWN COLLECTION.

CHAPTER 1

Ocracoke Lighthouse

Ocracoke Inlet, just south of Ocracoke Island, was the main and most important inlet on the North Carolina coast from the early 1700s to the mid-1800s. Through this inlet came our trade and contact with the outside world. Two-thirds if not three-fourths of the commerce of North Carolina passed through Ocracoke Inlet, not less than fifteen thousand sail of vessels annually (1824).[1] It was the only inlet that remained open and at the same site while others filled in and washed out again in another location.

1 *The* [Washington, N.C.] *Republican*, March 18, 1839.

In 1715 an act was passed by the colonial assembly to settle and maintain pilots at Ocracoke Inlet, "it being the only port with sufficient depth of water for ships of Burden between Topsail and the Virginia capes."[2] Though the inlet remained open, the sand bars and shoals shifted, making it dangerous to enter without the aid of a pilot.

Crossing the bar[3] at night was almost impossible, for, when there is no moon, these Outer Banks and surrounding waters are the darkest known to mankind. In 1789, because of the danger to shipping, the North Carolina General Assembly passed an act to erect a lighthouse on Ocracoke Island. On September 13, 1790, William Williams, John Williams, Joseph Williams, William Howard, Jr., and Henry Garrish deeded one acre of land to the State of North Carolina for the purpose of erecting the lighthouse.[4] The deed stated that if a lighthouse was not erected by January of 1801, the deed would be void.

However, in November of the same year, the federal government assumed the responsibility of construction and maintenance of lighthouses from the states. The construction of a light on Ocracoke Island was delayed,[5] and on March 28, 1792, it was ordered that the secretary of the treasury "inquire into, and report to congress at their next session, the expediency of erecting a light-house on Ocracoke Island, or elsewhere, near the entrance of Ocracoke Inlet, and an estimate of the probable expense."[6]

---

2 *Carteret County During the American Revolution (A Bicentennial Project of the Carteret County Bicentennial Commission)*

3 *bar*: a sand bar in the inlet that prevents vessels from passing.

4 Carteret County Register of Deeds, Beaufort, N.C.

5 David Stick, *Outer Banks of North Carolina* (Chapel Hill: The University of North Carolina Press, 1958), pp. 302-303.

6 *Ibid.*

Upon learning of the proposed construction of the light on Ocracoke Island, fifty-seven pilots, masters[7] of vessels, owners of vessels, and merchants trading in and out of the inlet got up a petition requesting it be built on Shell Castle Rock rather than on Ocracoke Island.

John Gray Blount and John Wallace operated a shipping company on Shell Castle, as well as a store, tavern, a lightering[8] business, and two large warehouses. On May 13, 1794, Congress approved construction of the lighthouse on Shell Castle, which was located just inside Ocracoke Inlet. On May 23, 1795, an invitation for bids was published in the *North Carolina Gazette*. The tower was to be constructed of wood and covered with shingles, pyramid-shaped, 54½ feet high, and set on a ten-foot-deep submerged stone foundation. There was to be a six-foot lantern and a three-foot dome. H. Dearborn was awarded the contract, and the lighthouse was completed in 1798 on a small piece of land deeded to the federal government by John Wallace and John Gray Blount in 1797.[9] A transcription of the deed found in an old unnumbered deed book, Carteret County, North Carolina, Register of Deeds, follows.

> Carteret County 29 November 1797
> John Gray Blount of Washington, NC and John Wallace of Shell Castle, NC to the United States of America for $200 Land for the purpose expressed in an Act of Assembly of the year 1794 entitled an Act for ceding to the United States the Jurisdiction of certain land on Shell Castle Island: in the Harbor of Ocracoke a certain lot on Shell Castle at the Easternmost end thereof and

---

7 ***master***: captain of a ship.

8 ***lightering***: the act of taking part or all of the cargo off a ship and into smaller boats to make it lighter in the water, enabling it to cross sand bars in the inlets.

9 *Ibid.*

The Outer Banks in 1861

Segment of "*J. H. COLTON'S TOPOGRAPHICAL MAP OF NORTH AND SOUTH CAROLINA. A LARGE PORTION OF GEORGIA & PART OF ADJOINING STATES. ENTERED ACCORDING TO ACT OF CONGRESS IN THE YEAR 1861 BY J.H. COLTON. NEW YORK PRINTED BY LANG & LAING, 1861.*"

MAP BY J.H. COLTON
COURTESY LIBRARY OF CONGRESS

to run along the rock to the Westward with Wallace Channel, seventy feet, then to beginning. With the stipulation that the U.S. shall not permit goods to be stored, a tavern to be kept, to be no retailed or merchandise to be carried on, on sd lot, or suffer any person to reside on or make that a stand from which they may either pilot or lighter vessels.

J.G. Blount
John Wallace

This 1798 light was soon rendered useless, as the shifting of sand bars and channels made it a distance of one mile from the main channel. Still the light remained in operation until it was destroyed by lightning on August 16, 1818. On May 15, 1820, fourteen thousand dollars was appropriated for a light vessel to be stationed in Ocracoke Inlet to replace the Shell Castle light. The light vessel proved unsatisfactory also and on May 7, 1822, twenty thousand dollars was approved for construction of a lighthouse on Ocracoke Island.[10]

The present lighthouse was constructed in 1823 by Noah Porter of Massachusetts at a cost of $11,359.35, which included the cost of the keeper's quarters, a one-story three-room brick house. The land on which the light was constructed was purchased from Jacob Gaskill for fifty dollars.[11]

The following is a description of navigational lights, etc.,

---

10 *Ibid.*

11 David Stick, *The North Carolina Lighthouses*, Raleigh, Division of Archives and History, North Carolina Department of Cultural Resources.

used by ships on entering Ocracoke Inlet.

> [Blount]-W.S.W. from Cape Hatteras, 8 leagues distant, is Ocracoke Inlet, on the bar of which are 9 feet of water; this bar is subject to change, and should not be entered without a pilot.
>
> At the entrance, on Ocracoke Island, a lighthouse is erected, exhibiting a revolving light, which you leave on your starboard hand entering the inlet. The time of each revolution is two minutes. It is elevated 75 feet above the water.
>
> A floating light is stationed within the point of the 9 feet shoal, near Teache's Hole Swash. She is moored in 2 fathoms water, with the light on Ocracoke bearing S.E. distance 2¾ miles, Shell Castle bearing

Teache's Hole, as seen looking southeast from Springer's Point on Ocracoke, in 1958.

PHOTOGRAPH BY M.V. WATSON. COURTESY NATIONAL PARKS SERVICE, CAPE LOOKOUT NATIONAL SEASHORE COLLECTION

S.W. ½ W., 4½ miles, and the light-boat at the S.W. Straddle W. by S. 9 miles. A bell will be toiled [tolled] at intervals in thick and foggy weather.[12]

12 Blount Papers, Raleigh, Division of Archives and History, North Carolina Department of Cultural Resources.

The lighthouse in 1893, a closeup taken from the larger photograph on Pages 24-25. Note the surveyor and one of his two cameras near the base of the lighthouse.

U.S. COAST GUARD

CHAPTER 2

Lighthouse Maintenance

The Treasury Department was the federal branch that was assigned responsibility for managing and maintaining lighthouses. The particulars that follow are from material found in the National Archives in Washington, D.C.[1] The style of the original documents has been preserved.

1854—At Ocracoke Island a fourth-order Fresnel fixed white light was substituted for the old reflecting

1 Records of The Bureau of Lighthouses and its Predecessors 1789-1939, Department of Transportation, Record Group 26, National Archives of the United States.

illuminating apparatus.

1855—Ocracoke. The keepers dwelling and tower at this station were thoroughly repaired in March 1855. The Ocracoke Channel light-vessel and Beacon Island light-house were intended as a range to cross the Ocracoke bar at night in safety.

Inconsequence of the formation of shoals inside the bar, that range never has been, nor can it be now obtained. Should it be attempted to cross the bar by bringing these lights in a direct line, a vessel would certainly strike on the reef, with every chance of inevitable destruction.

It is possible that a range might be obtained by having two light-vessels in place of the house and one light vessel, but the channel in which one of them would have to be moored is so subject to change that its continuance would, I fear, be of short duration. I would recommend that the two lights in question be discontinued, after sufficient notice to be given, and that the Ocracoke Channel light-vessel be stationed off the Northwest end of Royal Shoal, where a light is so much needed, until the screw-pile light-house, for which an appropriation has been made, is erected.

1856—New illuminating apparatus has been placed in the following light-houses, in this district, during the past year, viz. Hog Island, New Point, Comfort, Pools Island, Turkey Point, Sharps Island, Pamlico Point, Fishing Battery, Clay Island, Blackstone Island, the two at North Point, and Beacon Island.

1857—The Ocracoke Channel light-vessel, and the Beacon Island light-house, at the same place, have several times, been reported by this board as useless, and their discontinuance has been recommended. This recommendation is again respectfully renewed. DISCONTINUED "under the operation of the 3rd section of the act of Congress approved March 3, 1859."

1858—Beacon Island, inside of Ocracoke Inlet, brick tower, 38 feet elevation, built in 1853. Fixed, 6th-order lens light, refitted in 1855. Light on Keepers dwelling; designed as a range with light-vessel for the channel.

1860—New lanterns have been placed at Back River, Point Lookout, and Ocracoke light-houses. The substitution of Franklin for Valve lamps is going on.

1862—Ocracoke, tower standing, lens, &c., removed. [Editor's note: The Confederates removed the light from tower during the Civil War to prevent the Union ships from using it for navigation.]

1863—The light-house at Roanoke Marshes, Northwest

THE

MODERN LIGHT-HOUSE SERVICE

BY

ARNOLD BURGES JOHNSON,
CHIEF CLERK,
UNITED STATES LIGHT-HOUSE BOARD.

WASHINGTON:
GOVERNMENT PRINTING OFFICE.
1889.

Lighthouse keepers service manual, 1939

U.S. GOVERNMENT PRINTING OFFICE

Point of Royal Shoal, Croatan, Cape Lookout, and Ocracoke have been refitted and the lights re-exhibited.

1868—Ocracoke—A large portion of the tower has been re-cemented, and whitewashed two coats. Lantern and all wood in keepers dwelling and tower painted inside and out, two coats; lantern deck and sashes and frames repaired; stairways renovated extensively, putting in 33 feet of newel 14 inches diameter; one side of roof of keepers dwelling reshingled and other side repaired; fire-hearths and brick walks around the house relaid; plaster repaired in every room; also door, sashes, and hardware; floors repaired where necessary, and whitewashed.

1869—Ocracoke—The slight repairs required at this station have been made and it is now in fine order.

1883—Ocracoke, North side of Ocracoke Inlet, North Carolina. The old fence was removed and 1,200 feet of new paling fence substituted. The plaster in the dwelling was renewed, two new floors were laid, the lot was graded, and various minor repairs were made. The station is now in excellent order.

1899—Ocracoke, entrance to Ocracoke Inlet, N.C.

New model fourth-order lamps were supplied. Various repairs were made.

1903—Ocracoke, seacost of North Carolina.

In November 1902 a plank walk was laid from the dwelling to the tower.

1904—Ocracoke, seacoast of North Carolina.

A small wood shed was built in January. Some 324 running feet of fencing was erected. Various repairs were made.

On April 2, 1930, the lighthouse property on Ocracoke Island consisted of:

1 Lighthouse	$16,050
1 Oilhouse	500
1 Dwelling	5,670
1 Dwelling	7,000
1 Coal Shed	400
TOTAL	$29,620

The appraised value of the land was $1000.11[2]

2 Records in the custody of the Commissioner of the Revenue, in the Department of the Treasury.

Captain Joseph Merrit Burrus in full dress uniform. Burrus was the last keeper of Ocracoke Lighthouse, serving from 1929 to 1946. Note the lighthouse insignia on the cap.

PHOTO COURTESY GAYNELLE SPENCER TILLETT, DIGITAL IMAGE COURTESY CORE SOUND WATERFOWL MUSEUM AND HERITAGE CENTER

CHAPTER 3

Ocracoke Lightkeepers

The following is a list of the keepers appointed at Ocracoke between the lighthouse's being placed in service and the last keeper who retired in 1929, as well as information about them gleaned primarily from the United States Population Census.

OCRACOKE KEEPERS	ANNUAL SALARY	APPOINTED
Joshua Taylor		1823
Anson Harker		1824
John Harker	$400	Oct. 2, 1847
Thomas Styron	400	Sept. 1853
William J. Gaskill	400	Aug. 1860
Ellis Howard	560	1862

KEEPERS (cont.)	ANNUAL SALARY	APPOINTED
J. Wilson Gillikin	$560	1897
Tillmon F. Smith	552	1898
A.B. Hooper		1910
Wesley Austin		1912
J.M. Burruss		Oct. 1929

Joshua Taylor (or Tayloe)[1]
Collector of Customs
Superintendent of Ocracoke Lighthouse
1823-1829

Anson Harker[2]
Keeper of Ocracoke Lighthouse
1824-1846

First person designated as keeper of Ocracoke Lighthouse. Joshua Taylor retained position of superintendent.

John Harker
Keeper of Ocracoke Lighthouse
1847-1853

John Harker was appointed keeper of Ocracoke Lighthouse on 2 Oct. 1847 with a salary of $400 per year.[3] He is listed in the U.S. Federal Census of Ocracoke in 1850 as lightkeeper.

---

1 PUBLISHER'S NOTE: Joshua Taylor (or Tayloe) and his dates of service were not included in the original edition because, as the author wrote, "The records I've found do not cover the period prior to 1847." The information has since become available.

2 PUBLISHER'S NOTE: Likewise, the name of Anson Harker and his dates of service have been added to this edition.

3 Microfilm #1373-Lighthouse Keepers, National Archives of the United States.

John is listed as being 26 years of age. In the house with him were Elizabeth Harker 27, William Harker 29, and Harriet Harker 26. By 1860, the family was living in Straits District, Carteret County, North Carolina. The household members were the same as in 1850, which might mean they were all brothers and sisters, since there were no children listed as being born in the ten-year period. I found no marriage records for these people.

Thomas Styron
Keeper of Ocracoke Lighthouse
1853-1860

Thomas Styron was appointed keeper of Ocracoke Light house in September of 1853 to replace John Harker. He was keeper for seven years.[4] It is not certain which Thomas this was. In the 1850 census there was a Thomas Styron, age 53, and his son Thomas, age 29. Thomas Sr.'s occupation is listed as a boatman, and there is no occupation listed for Thomas Jr. Both are married and have a family. Both Thomas Styrons are listed in 1860, which was the year William Gaskill was appointed keeper. Neither Styron nor Gaskill was listed as a lightkeeper.

William J. Gaskill
Keeper of Ocracoke Lighthouse
1860-1862

William Gaskill was appointed keeper of Ocracoke Lighthouse in August of 1860 to replace Thomas Styron.[5] He was keeper for only two years before being replaced by Ellis Howard. He was listed in the 1860 census as being 48 years of age, married, wife Ann, age 45. Also listed were five children, Matilda 17, William 15, Robert 12, Zelpha 9, and Sam P. 6.

4 *Ibid.*
5 *Ibid.*

The two photos on these four pages were made as part of the May 24, 1893, survey of the Ocracoke Lighthouse reservation during the time of Keeper Ellis Howard. This photo was taken from "camera station no. 1" as noted on the plat. The surveyor and his camera can be seen at "camera station no. 2" near the base of the lighthouse itself, the keeper 's quarters and the trees. Whitewash was a mixture of lime, whiting, size, water,

etc. Traditionally on Ocracoke, molasses was added as well. As paint is used today, whitewash was used in past times to create a neat appearance on buildings.Whitewash also kept bugs from the trees. For a better appearance, whitewash on Ocracoke was applied to trees only to a height that matched that of the fence.

PRINT, OUTER BANKS HISTORY CENTER, MANTEO, N.C. ORIGINAL, NATIONAL ARCHIVES AND RECORDS AMINISTRATION, WASHINGTON, D.C.

Keeper Ellis Howard and family standing by the keeper's quarters. This photo was made from "camera station no. 2."

PRINT, OUTER BANKS HISTORY CENTER, MANTEO, N.C.
ORIGINAL, NATIONAL ARCHIVES AND RECORDS AMINISTRATION, WASHINGTON, D.C.

Enoch Ellis Howard
Keeper of Ocracoke Lighthouse
1862-1897

Ellis was appointed keeper of Ocracoke Light in 1862 with an annual salary of $560, which was still his annual income when he died in 1897,[6] thirty-five years later. Ellis Howard was born on Ocracoke on October 28, 1833, the son of Solomon Howard and Lovey Tolson. He married Cordelia Williams, also of Ocracoke. They had two children. Ellis remained keeper of the light until his death. He, his wife, and daughter are seen in the photographs of the keeper's quarters on pages 26-27.

J. Wilson Gillikin
Keeper of Ocracoke Lighthouse
1897-1898

I have found no information on Keeper Gillikin. He was keeper for less than a year and was not living at Ocracoke when the 1900 census was taken.

Keeper Gillikin made the first entry in the Lightkeepers Logbook found in the National Archives of History, Washington, D.C.[7] All entries were weather related except the following six.

June 6, 1897—Schooner *Cora* arrived from West Indies.
April 6, 1898—The schooner *S. Warren Hall* was wrecked just inside of the bar in Ocracoke Inlet about 2 Oclock yesterday loaded with shingles, from Georgetown, S.C. The crew was rescued by the crew of Portsmouth Life-Saving Station.
July 3, 1898—Keeper left to go to Baltimore to see doctor.
July 10, 1898—Keeper returned to station 7 am.
July 24, 1898—Keeper left station at 4 pm to go to Wash-

6 *Ibid.*

7 Lightkeeper's logbook, Ocracoke Station, Record Group 26, National Archives of the United States.

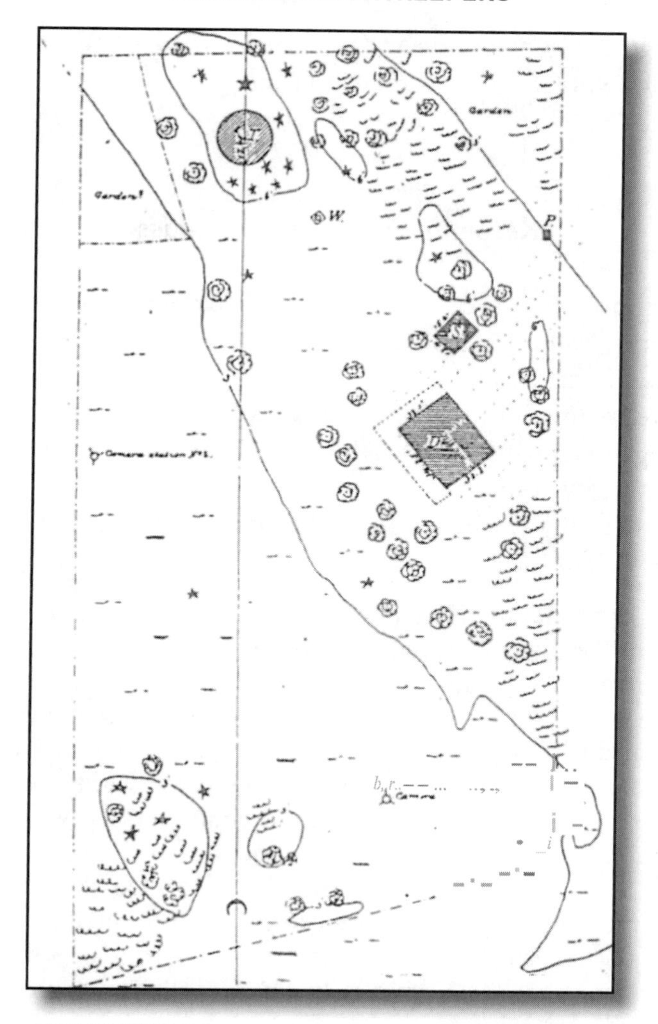

EXPLANATIONS: Datum = Assumed mean low water; T = Tower, brick; D = Dwelling, brick, roof shingle. Ht. floor 7.2'; S= Store house or shop, frame, shingleroof, wood foundation; W = Well, walled, inside diameter 2.9'; P = Privy, frame, wood foundation.

The actual 1893 physical survey showing the area enclosed by fence, site of the light, and location of buildings, high land, marsh, gardens, and trees.

RECORDS OF THE UNITED STATES COAST GUARD, GENERAL SERVICES AMINISTRATION, NATIONAL ARCHIVES & RECORDS ADMINISTRATION, WASHINGTON, D.C.

ington.

July 29, 1898—Keeper returned 6 am.

Tilmon F. Smith
Keeper of Ocracoke Lighthouse
1898-1910

Tilmon F. Smith was appointed keeper of Ocracoke Light in 1898. He is listed in the 1900 census as being 48 years of age. His wife was Sabra S., age 47. They had two boarders living in their home; Nora D. Smith, age 21, and Emagene Austin, age 13. Tilmon and Sarah had been married twenty-four years.

Entries by Keeper Smith other than weather and work done on station:[8]

Oct. 8,1898—The tender[9] *Violet* arrived at the station 3 pm. The mate of the tender delivered to the keeper 3 cord of wood and 2 tons of coal.

Oct. 15, 1898—The keeper whitewashes his cow stable and chicken house today.

Feb. 4, 1899—The lighthouse engineer visited the station today and took away the old lamps and left 3 new ones.

Feb.12, 1899—Snow storm. Keeper visited the light several times, from sunset to sunrise to keep the interior of the lantern glass clear of ice.

Jun. 8, 1899—Keeper sick, Mr. John Spencer substituted.

1900

Mar. 17-30—Keeper sick.

Jul. 25—Keeper received a telegram that his mother was dead

2pm—Left station 2:30 pm for Hatteras.

---

8 *Ibid.*

9 ***tender***: a small boat for carrying passengers and supplies to or from larger ships or lighthouses.

1901

Jun.—Tender *Holly* arrived in the harbor to work buoys.

Jul. 20—Keeper left to go to Washington to visit sick wife.

Jul. 26—Keeper is sick. Mr. George T. Willis substituted.

Jul. 28—Keeper is sick.

Oct. 26—Keeper left station to go to Rocky Mt. N.C.

1902

Jan. 1st. to Feb. 9th.—Keeper reported that he could not see reflection of search light from Diamond Shoal light.

May 1—Keeper left station today for medical treatment.

May 30—Keeper returned to station today.

Nov. 18—commenced building walk from dwelling to tower.

1903

May 4—Keeper and wife left at 11 am in answer to a telegram summoning them to their daughter in Washington, N.C.

May 12—Keeper returned to station 4 pm.

1905

Feb. 25—Keeper left 8:30 am to go to Bluff Shoal Light returned 4 pm.

A. B. Hooper
Keeper of Ocracoke Lighthouse
1910-1912

Hooper was appointed keeper of Ocracoke Lighthouse in 1910. He is listed as living at Ocracoke in 1910; his occupation is listed as lighthouse keeper. His wife was Mariah and they had been married for 25 years. Living with him were the following children: Richard, 23, son; Frederic, 20, son; Robert 15, son; and Hattie, 11, cousin.

Records in Logbook referring to Hooper were two

This photograph of "Captain Joe," as Joe Burruss was called, was made at the time of his retirement in 1946 and appeared in tbe *Raleigh News and Observer*. He is looking out over Silver Lake from the top of the lighthouse.

PHOTO COURTESY GAYNELLE SPENCER TILLETT, DIGITAL IMAGE COURTESY CORE SOUND WATERFOWL MUSEUM AND HERITAGE CENTER approvals for leave of absence, one on August 2, 1910, the other July 31, 1911.

Captain Leon Wesley Austin
Keeper of Ocracoke Lighthouse
1912-1929

Captain Austin was born at Hatteras, North Carolina, in 1864, the son of Isaac Farrow Austin and Sarah Ann Midgette. He married Isabelle Barnett, also of Hatteras. Wesley spent his late boyhood and early manhood on windjammers[10] plying the East Coast.

He entered the U.S. Lighthouse Service in 1885, serving on tenders as a freshman, then transferred to Cape Hatteras Lighthouse as third assistant keeper, where he served for eight years, earning a salary of $450 per year. In 1893, he was appointed first assistant keeper at Corolla, earning $500 a year.

Capt. Leon Wesley Austin was transferred to Ocracoke Station from Corolla Station November 28, 1912, when he was forty-eight years old. In 1913, he was promoted to keeper and transferred to Ocracoke Lighthouse.

He retired September 30, 1929, with more than forty-five years service with the Lightkeeper's Service. Wesley and Isabelle had four children and made Ocracoke their home when he retired. He died in 1941.

See Chapter Four for abstracts from Keeper Austin's log book.

Capt. Joe Burrus
Last Keeper of Ocracoke Lighthouse
1929-1946

Captain Burrus was the keeper of Ocracoke Lighthouse for sixteen years. He retired from the Lighthouse Service

10 *windjammer*: a sail ship.

The lighthouse in June 1936, during the time of Ocracoke's last keeper, Joe Burrus. These were a few of his daily views.

NATIONAL PARK SERVICE, CAPE HATTERAS NATIONAL SEAS

with forty-five years' service as keeper of lighthouses in Virginia and North Carolina. His first paycheck back in 1903 was thirty dollars per month.

Over the years he was stationed at Tangier, Virginia, Thimble Shoal, Virginia, and Diamond Shoal Lightship, Cape Lookout, Croatan, Oliver's Reef, Bluff Shoal, and Ocracoke, all in North Carolina. His service at Ocracoke was from 1929 to 1946. He was the last keeper of Ocracoke Lighthouse. There was no longer a need for a keeper after automation of the lights.

Joe was born at Hatteras, North Carolina, as was his wife, Eleanor Oden. They were the parents of six children and made Ocracoke their home after retirement.

Keeper Joe Burrus made but few entries in the logbook. It has been said that he refused to make entries because it was a waste of good time. He had more important things to do.

Opposite: Capt. Leon Wesley Austin was transferred to Ocracoke Station from Corolla Station November 28, 1912, when he was forty-eight. He retired from service September 30, 1929, after more than forty-five years with the Lightkeeper's Service.

COURTESY WARD GARRISH

CHAPTER 4

Keeper Wesley Austin's Logbook, 1912-29

The information recorded here was copied from microfilm from the National Archives in Washington, D.C. It covers the time period in which Wesley Austin was the Keeper of Ocracoke Lighthouse, 1912-1929. The logbook has an entry every day, which for the most part reports the weather of that day or that Captain Austin whitewashed the fence, tower, house, or outbuildings. I have tried here to report all other information as it was recorded in the logbook. I have copied it word for word as it was written, including misspelled words.

1912

Nov. 28th Reported for duty as Keeper of Ocracoke Light Station, Nov. 25, 1912—Wesley Austin, Keeper.

Dec. 13th At 2:30 am Vapor failed to burn, needling[1] would not do eny good. Substituted oil lamp untill sunrise.

1913

Jan. 3rd Had to take the vapor lamp out substitute oil lamp.

Feb. 4th Vaporizer leaked so bad had to substitute oil lamp.

Feb. 15th " " " " " " " " "

Feb. 16th " " " " " " " " "

Feb. 20th Chief construction enginer, H. B. Bowerman

---

1 ***needling***: the act of using a sharp object to clean a valve, which controls the flow of oil to a wick.

One of the tenders used to support supplies to lighthouses on the North Carolina coast. This is the tender that transported Captain Wesley Austin from Corolla Station to Ocracoke in 1912.

arrived at station at 3:30 pm on the 20th left at 8 am the 21st. for Cape Hatteras Light Station.

Mar. 4th Painted roof of dwelling.

Mar. 6th Light burned good til 1am-lam to sunrise falt.

Mar. 16th Painted window shutters on dwelling.

Mar. 29th Vapor light leaked bad substituted oil lamp at 7:45

May 28th Repair party arrived to station 2 pm and put cement coating on top of tower, repaired fence planks, walks and out buildings, left station.

July 10th The four masted schooner *V. Josephine* of Baltimore Md. went ashore at Ocracoke Inlet on the morning of July 10th 1913 at 4 am. Assistance was rendered by Ocracoke and Portsmouth Lifesaving Stations. Cause of Casualty—Ocracoke Light was mistaken for Bodie Island Light.

July 22nd From 3 to 3:45 am Light was very dim nozzle pretty stoped up.

Sept. 3rd Hunican on the night of the 2nd and morning of 3rd. From NE to SE blew and washed down part of the

fence, plank walks, slightly damaged by sea tide and did very much damage to trees inside reservation.[2]

Sept. 4th. Cleaning litter out of reservation—also on the 6, 7, 8, 9, & 10th.

Sept. 11th Repaired water closet.

Sept. 13th Repaired plank walk

Sept. 15th Repaired fences

Sept. 17th Touched up dwelling with whitewash

Oct. 2nd Inspected this date, found in good condition.

Oct. 16th Tender *Holly* delivered anual supplies to station. Keeper delivered to tender *Holly* 120 oil cans and 2-class can buoy.

Oct. 24th Referring to report of service rendered by you during the storm of Sept. 2 & 3, 1913[3], for preserving the government property under your charge and in giving shelter to the residents of Ocracoke Island, who were driven from their homes by the high tides, you are commended for the service rendered on the occasion in question, which fact will be noted on the records as part of your official history.

—Through, Commissioner of Lighthouses.

Oct. 25th Commenced to whitewash outside of tower. worked 2hr

26th " " " " " " " worked 8 hrs.

27th " " " " " " " " 3 hrs.

Nov. 1st Finished scraping and whitewashing out side of tower

3rd Painted outside of lantern of tower

4th Painted lantern deck of tower

6th Whitewashed fence

Dec. 2nd Sub oil lamp, vaporizer leaked at joint, also 2, 3,

---

2 PUBLISHER'S NOTE: The infamous Sept. 3, 1913, hurricane washed away bridges, damaged crops and property, and shipwrecked the 325-foot-long *George W. Wells*, one of the largest wooden ships ever built, on Ocracoke Island. Statewide, the hurricane killed five people and caused $3 million in damage (in 1913 dollars) but Ocracoke may have been hardest hit. For a time it was feared the entire population of the island had been killed.

3 See previous note.

4, 5, 6th.
11th Tender *Holly* supplyed 3 tons coal, 2 cords wood.
12th Light burned good all night—new preheater.

1914
Jan. 3rd One redhead killed against tower.
Feb. 23rd Repair crew arrived at station at 8 am to build new oil house.
Mar. 10th Painted outside kitchen wall
16th Painted boxing around eves of dwelling.
17th Painted outside of dwelling.
26th Cleaning old paint off of inside of lantern.
Apr. 6th Whitewashed inside of tower.
17th Painted stairway inside of tower
Jun. 5th Filled in yard with mud from ditch to hold the grass in back yard.
26th Tender *Holly* delivered annual supplies.
Jul. 7th Keeper left station 6 am on leave of absence
15th Keeper returned to station 10 am from leave 8 days 4 hours.
31st Station inspected, found in excellent condition.

Aug. 1914
EFFICENCY STARS—AUG. 18, 1914
KEEPER OCRACOKE LIGHT STATION
You are informed that you have been awarded an efficency star, you are therefore entitled to wear the efficency star for the succeding fiscal year beginning July 1st, 1914. Shall be worn in a manor describeed in the uniform manuel.

Tender *Holly* delivered two cords of wood and three tons of coal to station at 3 pm.

1915
Mar. 22nd Repair party arrived at station 8 am, minor repairs and left station at 4 pm.
June 1st Copy; Lighthouse Inspector, Baltimore, Md.
Sir; I write to tell you there are some complaints with the captains of the vessels now trading from Ocracoke

in regards to the beacon light no. 1155, Swash Channel, not showing effecient light at night and that a white light would give better satisfaction.

Wesley Austin, Keeper

June 7th Inspected station—condition very good, *King*
July 3rd Keeper left station at 2 pm returned at 5 pm
12th William Venson arrived to station at 1 pm installed recording thermometer in tower and left station at 10:30 am
Aug. 13, 1915.
Sept. 3rd Needled lamp at 8 pm.
18th Tender *Laurel* delivered supplies to station.
20th Painted outside lantern of tower and lantern deck.
Oct. 11th Painted inside of lantern of tower and lantern floor
Dec. 17th At 5:45 am vapor lamp worked bad, was necessary to substitute oil lamp until daylight.
24th Keeper left station at 5:45 pm to attend church, returned to station at 7:05 pm.

1916
Mar. 4th Alarm bell called at 3:35 am, light was all right. Needled lamp and adjusted the alarm.
Apr. 3rd Repair party arrived to station at 8am. tuck out part off plank walks and kitchen.
4th Put in forms for concreet walks
5th Repaired kitchen and made forms for top of cistern
6th Repaired kitchen and concreet top of cisterrn
7th Built new privey and concreet foundation
8th Building concreet walks
10th Taking up plank walks for cencreet
11th Building concreet walks and closet in tower
12th Building concreet walks
13th Repair party finished work, left station 9:30 am
14th Cleaning reservation
15th Cleaning up reservation
16th Sunday
17th Whitewashing inside walls of tower
19th Painting outbuildings of station
21st Taking out forms around walks
22nd Cleaning reservation

23rd Sunday
24th Painting outbuildings
25th Painting closet in tower
26th Painting porch to kitchen
27th Whitewashing outside of tower
29th Cleaning elluminating apparatus
30th Sunday
May 23rd Fixing chicking lot
(all other days spent cleaning painting & white washing, house, fence and tower).
31st Painted hot house
Jun 1st Pollashed elluminating apparatus
10th Pollashed brass articles, lamps etc.
15th No lights visible except-Swash and Cockle shoal Beacons
16th Wind and rain badly beat off whitewash on outside wall of tower.
18th Keeper left station at 10:30 am to attend church, returned 12 noon.
21st SW Point, Bluffshoal and Beacon vissible
25th Keeper left station at 2:30 pm returned 3 pm
28th Tender *Laural* delivered annual supplies
29th Stacking up annual supplies and taking inventory
30th Made out annual property return
Jul 4th Wind and rain badly beat off thermomoner pen caught—behind bad from 7 pm to 10 pm
5th Keeper sick all day no work done
6th Cleaned up in tower
6th Keeper left station 8:30 am returned June 20 at 12:30 pm period of absence 12 days. and 4 hours for medical treatment.
7th Keeper left station at 6:35 am on leef July 7, 1916
8th Worked on the tower burnt oil lamp
9th Act keeper left station at 10:45 to attend church returned 2:15.
11th Tuck out oil lamp
12th Went to the post office for the mail
14th Hot and sultry all day—no work done
16th Left station 10:30 to attend church returned 4:15
17th Left station 3:30 for the mail returned 5:30
19th Rain and win storm from NE vapor bad from 6:30-7:30
24th House open for ventilation

July 7 Keeper lift station at 6:35 am on leave of absense, returned to station July 25 at 1:30 pm—period of absence 15 days, 6 hours and 55 min.

26th Keeper returned to station July 26, 1916 at 1:30 pm

Aug 1st Cutting weeds around fence

2nd Cutting grass inside reservation

4th Scowerd staresteps in tower

6th Keeper left station at 10:30 to attend church, returned 12 noon.

Aug 7th Scowerd porch floors of dwelling

9th United States Coast and Geodetic survay put in bench mark at tower door.

Undated photograph by unknown photographer.

AUTHOR COLLECTION, DIGITAL IMAGE COURTESY OF CORE SOUND WATERFOWL MUSEUM AND HERITAGE CENTER

1917

Jan 15th Owing to bad weather no work don at station at 7:20 pm lamp worked so bad tuck out vaporizer and connection relief valve to lamp. light extinguished 30 minutes.

Feb 2nd Snowing, fresh breeze NW pm snowing fresh gale NW

3rd Owing to bad weather no work done today. lantern of tower sweted and frozed untill all inside of lantrn was iced over.

4th Keeper sick with rheumatism all day

5th Inside of lantern iced over tonight

Apr. 12th Painted black outside lantern of tower
13th Asst. supt inspected station at 4 pm
16th Put in telegraph poles inside reservation
Sep. 2nd Alarm bell called and going in tower found the lamp enveloped in red flame, turned oil off and needled lamp then the lamp burned fare untill sunrise.
Oct 3rd Installed telephone in office today
Dec 26th Rain and snow fresh breeze NE
29th Snow and rain to severe snow storm fresh gale NW
30th Snowing
31st Coast Gard telephone inspector visited station at 3:36 pm

1918
Jan 1st Clear light breeze NW freezing weather
2nd Snowing, light breeze NE freezing
20th Snow
Apr 1st By order—clock turned ahead one hour 2 am March 31st.

1919
Feb 3rd Coast Guard Supt. visited station at 4:45 pm
Norfolk Va. June 12, 1919, 8 pm to all Coast Guard Stations from No. 101 to 191 . . . Coast Guard Stations, Lighthouse Keepers, and all petroles along the coast from Cape Henry to Cape Fear, *Keep bright lookout for submarines* for all scho rig, schooners, steam or sail painted gray, and any news from conserning subject. Keep the department informed. *This subject very important.*

signed,
Capt. Commandont
5th Navel District

RECORD OF ABSENCE
1919 WESLEY AUSTIN left station 25 times; once to attend public speaking, once to carry daughter to Hatteras,

once on annual leave, and 22 times to attend church.

1920
May 4th Keeper worked on his motor boat
22nd Making pickets to replace fence
25th Put in nine fence post today
26th Put in 6 fence post and one rail today
27th Put in 7 fence post
28th Made 79 pickets for fence
Jun 1st Put up guttering on dwelling
8th 75 pickets today
9th 60 pickets today
10th Made 2 gates for fence
Jul 14th Tender *Laurel* delivered supplies today
Aug 11th Light out of commission, substituted old oil lamp

1921
Aug 11th—Keeper left station at 7 am to meet daughter at Hatteras
Aug 12th—Showing visitors in tower
Aug 12th—Schooner *Message of Peace* marroned in Ocracoke Inlet just below Teaches Hole. Bouy Haling Port Nassau, NJ
Nov. 11th—American Flag Flown On Ocracoke Light Station in honor of Americans dead, from Sunrise to Sunset

1923
July 27th—Keeper stuck a 20 penny nail in bottom of foot, making a painful wound about l pm. 28, 29, 30, 31, not able to work because of foot
Aug 10th—Keeper left on leave today

1925
Aug. 23—Four masted schoonor *Victoria S.* stranded on Ocracoke Roads about 1 am—in part from Georgetown SC to New York loaded—Pine lumber. Keeper Feb 11, 1921 Called by keeper C. G. Stationn on telephone—notifed light was out—hurridely going in tower reheated lamp 10 min—relit the light at 3:05 am—light extinguished from 2:15 to 3:05 am time extinguished about

The schooner *Victoria S.*, shipwrecked on Ocracoke in 1925.
PHOTOGRAPHER UNKNOWN

50 min—caused by nozzle stoping up alarm bell failed to call at proper time.

INSPECTIONS
Inspector declared station in Excellent Condition;
1914 Jan 18, Jun 7, Oct 18, Apr 10, Sept 25,
1917 Apr. 13, Sept. 3,
1918 March 8th
1919 May 17th

TELEGRAM
Baltimore Md.
Aug. 5, 1920
To Wesley Austin
Ocracoke, NC
20 days leave with substance, government expence approved.
Dillon
received 9:30 pm

TELEGRAMS
Department of Commerce

Send to Port Captain
Ocracoke, NC July 24, 1924
Buoy Dept.

Portsmouth, Va
All buoys relieved around Ocracoke, will load oil dryms and leave Friday enroute Washington, Kindly

Ocracoke, Oct. 18, 1927
All buoys releived around Ocracoke, complete work as signed necessary proceed Washington for coal—leave Ocracoke Wednesday-winds and sea permitting Kindly

Coast Survey Washingtonn DC
Ocracoke, Aug 21, 1927
Arrived Ocracoke twentieth. Moore

Port Captain
Ocracoke, NC July 1925
Lighthouse Dept. Portsmouth Va.
Juniper arrived Ocracoke Wednesday night condition unsuitable for buoy work—report juniper, Baltimore office

Portsmouth Bouy Dept.
Keeper Light Station
Portsmouth Va to Ocracoke Light Station, Ocracoke NC
Lighthouse tender *Speedwell* will arrive Ocraacoke Bar weather permitting, Tuesday morning Nov. 20—Make arrangement local pilot to meet pilot acknolage. Almy

This photograph is an aerial view looking from the Ocracoke Lighthouse toward Silver Lake. It was taken by Aycock Brown in the 1950s. The docks of the World War II Navy base can be seen at the top of the photo.

OUTER BANKS HISTORY CENTER, MANTEO, N.C.
AYCOCK BROWN COLLECTION

Baltimore Md.
July 8, 1921
Keeper Ocracoke Light Stationn, Ocracoke, NC reply to letter of June 17, Relative Schooner—*Carroll A. Dearing.*[4]
King

To Supt of Lighthouses
Ocracoke Light Station
Baltimore, MD
July 9, 1921
Reply to letter June 17th 1921—relative *Carroll A Derring*[5] forwarded by mail. Keeper

WESLY AUSTIN, Keeper of Ocracoke Light Station was retired from active duty in the Light House Service with the close of business Sept. 30th 1929 after 45 years, 3 months service.
Oct 11th 1929—J. M. BURRUS reported for duty at this Station today.
Oct 29th 1929—Light changed to electric.

4 PUBLISHER'S NOTE: The *Carroll A. Deering*, a five-masted schooner, famously ran aground off Cape Hatteras in late January 1921. Its crew was never found, nor, despite a lengthy investation, was any explanation discovered.
5 See note above.

Ocracoke Preservation Society, Inc.

P.O. Box 491, Ocracoke, North Carolina 27960-0456

FEB 8,1989

U.S. COAST GUARD
OCRACOKE, NC 27960

OCRACOKE PRESERVATION SOCIETY HAS IN IT'S POCESSION FOR SAFE KEEPING, EIGHT SECTIONS, (FOUR WINDOWS) FROM THE OCRACOKE LIGHTHOUSE, THAT WERE REMOVED WHEN THE NEW WINDOWS WERE INSTALLED.

Ellen F. Cloud
ELLEN F. CLOUD
TRUSTEE

Received by D.W. Gascalle [illegible] Date 09 FEB 89
I hereby sign for this particular reciept.

The U.S. Coast Guard asked for a signed statement to the effect, that we had the windows, which relieved them from responsibility. This is a copy of the statement.

CHAPTER 5

The Great Window Heist

A FIRST-PERSON ACCOUNT

The Ocracoke Lighthouse and the structures within the compound were on the National Register of Historical Places long before the Village of Ocracoke became an Historical District. Approximately thirty-two thousand people visit this historical station annually. It is owned by the U.S. Coast Guard (USCG), which is responsible for the operation and maintenance of the lighthouse. The keeper's quarters are used by the National Park Service, which has the responsibility for the maintenance and upkeep in accordance with the terms of a written agreement with the U.S. Coast Guard. In 1987, the National Park Service (NPS) determined that the keeper's quarters needed major rehabilitation, and by 1990 had expended $278,000 to rehabilitate the interior of the structure. During this time several inspections were made of the lighthouse and it was found in need of immediate preservation work to stabilize its deteriorating condition. As a result of a Bicentennial Lighthouse Grant of seventeen thousand dollars, the NPS initiated an "Historic Structures Report" to assess the structure's condition, document historic fabric, and develop a scope of work.

Near the lighthouse is a small generator house, which holds the generator that keeps the lighthouse in operation when there is a power outage. Because Ocracoke gets its power from Virginia, the island is often without electricity; if anything happens anywhere down the line, we who are at the end of the line lose power. The lighthouse had continued to glow with or without power for 165 years until 1988, when the tired, worn out generator ceased to work. The U.S. Coast Guard decided not to replace it, as it would be less costly to install battery driven navigational lights on the handrails that encircled the lamp of the tower. This was done by drilling holes through the structure near the base, through which cables could be run that would operate the lights by batteries. Not only was it unsightly, it added seriously to the weakening of the structure.

The presence of the light from Ocracoke Lighthouse had given the residents of Ocracoke, as well as the captains of ships off shore, a feeling of security that even we were unaware of until the first power outage. None of us realized that, when an outage occurred, our first reaction was to immediately look in the direction of the lighthouse. A feel-

Light in Ocracoke lighthouse, 1936

NATIONAL PARK SERVICE, CAPE HATTERAS NATIONAL SEASHORE

ing of desertion and insecurity must have swept the island, for the power outage was the topic of the next day's conversation. The two small battery-operated lights that had been installed on the rail were on and the lighthouse was in darkness. The sight was viewed with anger and disbelief.

In February of 1989 a contract was put in operation to paint the lighthouse and repair the windows and door. The old wood-clad windows were removed and vinyl Andersen windows with snap-in muntins[1] (which are in violation of the Secretary of the Interior's Standards for historic structures) were installed.

Upon learning of this, I contacted two friends, who joined me, and promptly took action, demanding that the contractor cease work. The contractor disregarded our demands, but we were able to make a quick inspection of the work being done. Not only were the windows a violation by style and material, but they were not large enough for the

1 *muntins*: frames for holding the glass panes of a window.

opening in the structure! The openings had been framed up with 4x4 material to make the windows adaptable. Inquiring about the old windows, we learned that they were to be sent to Portsmouth, Virginia, to be destroyed and were at this time inside the ground level of the lighthouse.

We left the premises in order to make some phone calls and inform the proper authorities. We talked to the U.S. Coast Guard, National Park Service, State Historical Preservation Society, and Congressman Walter P. Jones's office. All agreed that these acts were in violation of Section 106 of the National Historical Preservation Act of 1966.

These photos show the battery-operated navigational lights which were installed on the handrails that encircle the lamp itself. To cut costs, the U.S.C.G. installed these lights, instead of replacing the worn-out generator.

PHOTOGRAPHS BY SALLY NEWELL

This photograph shows the vinyl Andersen windows with snap-in muntins that had been installed in place of the original six-over-six wooden windows. These vinyl windows were in violation of the Secretary of the Interior's Standards for historic structures.

PHOTOGRAPH BY SALLY NEWELL

In one of those phone calls, I was made aware of a letter dated May 27, 1987, two years prior, from the Department of Cultural Resources in Raleigh, North Carolina, to the United States Coast Guard in Portsmouth, Virginia, part of which follows:

> We seriously question the need to replace all windows and frames as specified in Section 8G. Our photographs of Ocracoke Lighthouse indicate that the existing wood windows and frames are in fair-to-good condition. The total replacement of all window frames and sash with new vinyl-clad or aluminum-clad units with snap-in muntins would be in violation of the Secretary of the Interior's Standards for use in either the door or windows of the Ocracoke Lighthouse.
>
> We recommend that each existing window frame and sash be carefully inspected for its condition. Any deteriorated elements of the window frames, such as sills, stops, jams, and lintels should be repaired or replaced to match the existing detailing. All sash which are in sound condition should be repaired and glazed as needed. Frames or sash which are too deteriorated to be repaired should be replaced with new frames or sash which have been milled or fabricated to match the existing ones. Any new replacement sash should be of true six-light construction, and identical to the existing sash. Snap-in muntins are not acceptable.

Realizing that the workmen at the lighthouse at that very moment were in direct violation of all official instructions for the project and that we had confirmation of this fact, we returned to the lighthouse to inspect the windows which had been removed from the structure. Upon arrival we found the door of the lighthouse had been secured by twisting wire around the latch. With much protest from the contractor, we opened the door and found the windows to be in excellent condition. We proceeded to take the win-

THEY'RE OURS
AND WE'RE
TAKING THEM
BRINGA
BACKA MY
WINDOWS!
Ellen Marie

The Great Window Heist

This cartoon by Butsie Brown was circulated through the village of Ocracoke for months after the incident and was sold in some of the gift shops and the Art Co-Op.

ORIGINAL ARTWORK BY BUTSIE BROWN

dows to our vehicle in order to hold them for safekeeping, ignoring the demands of the contractor to put them back.

Realizing, as we drove off, the seriousness of removing federal property without permission, we decided to call all authorities, both state and federal, to inform them of our act and demand they take action at once to render support and cease the destruction of this historical structure.

By late afternoon a meeting had been arranged for the following Wednesday with the National Park Service, our Hyde County Commissioner, and several U.S.C.G. Officers, including Commander Malrose and Lt. McCaffrey, both of Cleveland, Ohio, who had the contract with the civilian contractor. I had had several conversations earlier in the day with Malrose or McCaffrey. I felt they were neither cooperative nor courteous; on two occasions they refused to take my calls.

At the meeting, Commander Malrose and Lt. McCaffrey, who had flown in from Cleveland, heard our complaints and were informed of the seriousness of disregarding the regulations for compliance with Section 106 of the Advisory Council. This law was clearly explained by a specialist on restoration of historical structures at this meeting.

After hearing our complaints, Commander Malrose agreed to have windows milled like the old ones to replace the vinyl ones and to purchase a generator and remove the lights on the rail.

In April of the following year, after seeing no activity that would make the situation right, I called Commander Malrose, who denied making such agreements. He said he planned to do nothing until the summer of 1990. He was told that we wanted the lights removed before August 7th, which had been designated as National Lighthouse Day, and that we could live with the windows until after that date. His reply was short and to the point, saying; "I wish you luck. I have no plans for the near future to do any of this work."

I called Congressman Jones's office, and talked with Mr. Floyd Lupton, who said he would get right on it. At 5:30 p.m., Mr. Lupton called me back to inform me that a generator would be purchased and shipped that day. The battery-operated lights would be off before August 7th. He stated that the windows would take longer because they had to be milled.

As promised by Congressman Jones's office, the generator was replaced and the lights removed from the rail, though not in time for the August 7th celebration, for the generator house had to be restored. The old original windows have now been reworked and are back in place within the structure. The National Park Service is to be given credit for this, for it was their restoration department that restored the windows, but I must add that the United States Coast Guard paid the bill.

This act was a startling realization of the importance of getting the lighthouse placed under the control of the National Park Service. Several contacts have been made in an attempt to achieve this goal. The Coast Guard is anxious to transfer the structure to the National Park, but they must retain ownership of the light or lens at the top, since all aids to navigation are their responsibility. The National Park wants the ownership of the structure but must wait and go through all the governmental red tape necessary for such a transfer.

I in no way mean to criticize the U.S. Coast Guard, for they play a most important part in the lives of all the Bankers. They risk their lives every day in order to save others. Most of the male population of Ocracoke has served in or been part of the Coast Guard or Life-Saving Service, or in

Ocracoke Lighthouse as it is today.

some way been helped by the service. It is a branch of the military service that we hold in great admiration and pride.

The Coast Guard's responsibility is to save lives and not historical structures. It is for this reason we recommend the lighthouse be placed under the control of the National Park, whose main priority is the restoration of such structures.

As of this printing the U.S. Coast Guard and Cape Hatteras National Seashore are still negotiating the possible transfer of title of this, the oldest lighthouse on the Outer Banks of North Carolina.[2]

Ellen Fulcher Cloud
December 1992

---

2 PUBLISHER'S NOTE: Having succeeded in seeing that proper replacements were made for the lighthouse windows and generators, the author and fellow islanders ultimately would gain another victory. This one would take longer, however. Ownership of and responsibility for the lighthouse finally would be transferred from the Coast Guard to the National Park Service in 1999.

Acknowledgments

The list of people to be thanked for the publication of this booklet is endless. First on the list is Sally Newell, who was so determined that I publish this book that she established Live Oak Publications. Thanks to Willis Slane, Agnes Wren, Paulette Chitwood, and Jennie Micket of Live Oak Publications for their support and work in getting it published. Thanks to Chief Peter Stone of the United States Coast Guard for his support during the "Window Heist" and for not having us arrested, and to Tom Hartman and Bebe Woody of the Cape Hatteras National Park for backing us all the way. Thanks to Mr. William F. Sherman of the Civil Reference Branch, National Archives, for his help in providing much needed research material for this project. Again, a special thanks to Paulette Chitwood for sharing her knowledge of design and layout and the many hours she spent working on this project. Thanks to my mother who never complained when she was left to watch TV alone while I buried myself in papers. To all my friends who kept insisting that this booklet needed to be wtitten, thanks!

PART II

THE OLD SALTS

Old Salt, 1995, original cover
(Photo of Capt. James Horatio Williams, Philadelphia, 1887,
courtesy of Elizabeth Howard)

Ocracoke Island
Pamlico Sound
Atlantic Ocean
Ocracoke
Silver Lake
Ocracoke Inlet

PHOTO BY M.V. WATSON, 1955,
COURTESY CAPE HATTERAS NATIONAL SEASHORE, NATIONAL PARK SERVICE

Preface

December 1992

In the 1950s, Ocracoke Island became so attractive to tourists that the state decided we needed paved roads and ferry service to the mainland. Those improvements, of course, began to change our island from the quaint little fishing village that people remembered to the tourist area it is at this time. The changes have been so rapid and so complete that I felt it was time to remind the people of Ocracoke, as well as the visitors to the island, that we are and always have been more than just a tourist attraction. The seafaring history of Ocracoke goes back long before the days of commercial fishermen.

In general conversation, I have discovered that few residents or visitors know anything of the seafaring history of Ocracoke. I feel it is imperative that this history be remembered, that something needs to be done to acknowledge this rich heritage of our forefathers. Therefore, I am attempting to put together here a brief history so that this information will be available to all.

This booklet is an attempt to remind Ocracokers of who we are, to remind us of what we want to be, to help us put our priorities in order and to stop and look at where we are going.

ELLEN FULCHER CLOUD

Jamie Styron, local fisherman, and Bill Rothrock, visitor.

PHOTOGRAPH COURTESY CLARA JACKSON

CHAPTER 6

Old Salt

Old Salt is a description, or name, given to men of the sea, men who make their living working on the water and risk their lives every day doing so. They respect the sea, the weather, and God. God created the sea and gave it a mind of is own. It can be beautiful, calm, peaceful, rough, angry, cruel, life-taking and life-giving.

It takes a special breed of men to survive all the elements of the sea, a man with salt water in his veins, one who can listen to the ocean and know when a storm is brewing. The ocean talks to those who respect her. She talks in ways that only *Old Salts* understand. She whispers on calm days, showing only slight swells offshore and waves quietly rolling in to shore. When there is a storm brewing south of us, she lets us know by roaring loud enough to be heard even at night while one lies sleeping. She pops and snaps loudly as the waves break and crash upon the beach.

It has been written that "she takes care of her own." And indeed she does. Through the years she has deposited on the beaches of these Outer Banks just about anything that can be imagined—lumber to build a home, fruit for Christmas, barrels of pork, flour, and molasses, cases of canned goods, furniture, coins, horses, even an automobile.[1] She takes care of her own, and when the time is right she claims her own. She reaches out and takes what is hers, be it the shore line, a sand dune, a house, a lighthouse, a ship, or a life.

Then one may ask, why do men continue to risk their lives this way? It was "born in them," a local would say. They have salt water in their blood. It is a breed that knows no other world. Take one of these men, put him on the mainland behind a desk or in a factory assembly line or in any other job away from the sea, and he would not survive.

Every man on Ocracoke Island from 1715, when the first pilots were assigned here, until the 1960s made his living from the sea except for an occasional teacher or clerk. They neither knew nor wanted any other life. The sea took many of them but they died doing what they loved best.

Today it would appear that men of Ocracoke no longer "go down to the sea," but this is not true. Many people who have moved here are now "local" and hold jobs, own businesses, or are retired. These men do not make their living from the sea. But if you happen to be around Silver Lake ("the Creek")[2] early in the morning you will see, ever so

---

1 Tbe schooner *John I. Snow*, wrecked on Portsmouth Beach January 14, 1907, had on board an automobile that was salvaged by a resident of the island.

2 "The Creek" is now called Silver Lake. Until World War II, it was a creek too shallow for boats. At the beginning of the war, the Creek was dredged to make a harbor for ships when a Navy base was built in the area of the public docks and parking lot.

often, an open boat possibly loaded with crab pots or nets, with one man aboard slowly making its way out of "the Ditch.[3] Soon he will be at his fishing grounds, where he will work at his own pace, with no one looking over his shoulder, no schedule to keep, salt spray in his face, and a face of complete peace.

There are only a few who make their living solely from the sea, but there are those who wear many hats, only one of which is that of a seaman. Young men had to leave the island in the 1960s to seek employment because commercial fishing was on the decline and there was no other means of employment. Most have returned now. Many have retired from the Coast Guard, the Army Corps of Engineers, or tug boating, and they now work on the ferries and are also commercial fishermen. Others own and operate their own businesses and still find time to fish with nets, crab pots, etc. This is how they survive the stress and confusion of the other jobs. They "go down to the sea." If you should happen to be around when one of these men returns to his dock, ask his name. I guarantee he will be an O'Neal, Gaskill, Garrish, Ballance, Fulcher, Spencer, Styron, or one of the other names descended from one of those who settled here in 1715.

Under this cover, I am making an attempt to preserve some of the history of the seafaring residents of Ocracoke Island and make available to our grandchildren and visitors alike information about the great part these men had in the history of this island, this state, and this country. It is my wish that this book be a memorial to their existence, the Old Salts.

---

3 'The Ditch" is the narrow entrance to the harbor. The original name for the Creek was "Cockle Creek." To the natives of the island it is, and always will be, "The Creek" and "the Ditch."

One-room shacks such as these were the living quarters of the pilots.

DRAWING BY ELLEN FULCHER CLOUD

CHAPTER 7

THE PILOTS

Ocracoke Island was not known to be inhabited before the pilots came, but it was used by residents of the mainland for grazing cattle, horses, and sheep. Fernefould Green was one of those permitted to do so. The island was a perfect pasture that needed no fences, for it was surrounded by water that made it impossible for animals to wander off.

From The Colonial Records of North Carolina (Second Series, Vol. VII, Records of the Executive Council 1664-1734) comes the following:

> Petition to Governor and Council
> {1706}
> To the Honorable the Governor and Council The

Cattle and horses roamed free on Ocracoke Island until the 1950s.

PHOTOGRAPHS COURTESY ELLEN ROBINSON, DIGITAL IMAGES COURTESY CORE SOUND WATERFOWL MUSEUM AND HERITAGE CENTER

petition of Fernefould Green humly showeth That whereas your honors humble orator having a great desire to settle a stock upon the Banks at or near Ocracoke Inlett and having understood that the honorable Governor hath given orders that the said places should not be settled by any straingers but what are of good fame, least any harme should befale any of her Majestys subjects that should through Chance be Cast away there, Therefore your humble Orator shall as in duety bound for ever pray, etc.

Fernefold Green[1]

In 1715, the colonial assembly passed an act to settle and maintain pilots at Ocracoke, it being the only port with sufficient depth of water for ships of burden between Topsail (now Beaufort, North Carolina) and the Virginia Capes. It was the responsibility of the pilots to guide ships

1 Permission was granted by the Executive Council.

PILOTS[1]

These pilots' names were found in The State Records, Colonial Records, Blount Papers, and Records of Deeds in Carteret, Hyde, and Currituck counties.

John Bragg
Jesse Bragg
Christopher O'Neal
John O'Neal
William O'Neal
Horatio Williams
James Wahab
George Dixon
Francis O'Neal
Henry Salter
James Styron
Robert Gaskill
Francis Jackson
Benjamine Jackson
Isaac Jackson
John Howard
Thomas Oliver
Thomas Nelson
Adam Gaskins
John Gaskins
John Williams
Joseph Williams

1 List of names constituted a chapter in *Old Salt*.

across the bar[2] at Ocracoke Inlet and into the deep waters of the sound.

These first settlers, the pilots, were squatters on land owned by the Lords Proprietors. They kept to themselves and avoided the outside world, except for job-related contacts. They were called "Wild and Barbarous, Slovenly Brutes, Ignorant Beast" and worse. They did not like intruders and civilization passed them by. Most of the people who saw the island were eager to move on, as the fear of coastal storms and the shallow sounds made settlement very difficult. The greatest fear was of the pirates who often used Ocracoke as a gathering place.

The pilots, with their leather-looking skin, deep-set, squinting eyes, thick beards, and wrinkled brows caused by too much sun and salt, were not a welcoming group to say the least. They were on Ocracoke to do a job, and do a job they did, above and beyond their sworn duty.

2 *bar*: a sand bar in the inlet that prevents vessels from passing.

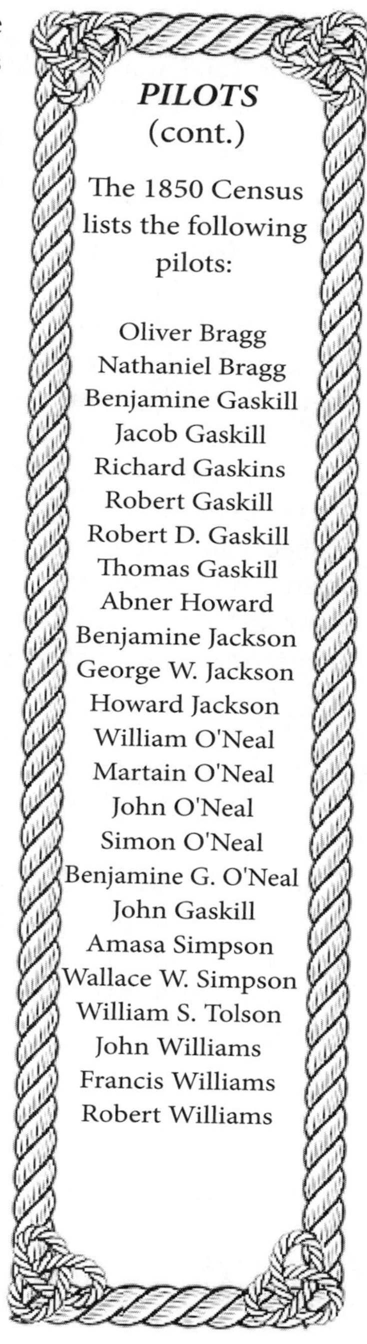

PILOTS
(cont.)

The 1850 Census lists the following pilots:

Oliver Bragg
Nathaniel Bragg
Benjamine Gaskill
Jacob Gaskill
Richard Gaskins
Robert Gaskill
Robert D. Gaskill
Thomas Gaskill
Abner Howard
Benjamine Jackson
George W. Jackson
Howard Jackson
William O'Neal
Martain O'Neal
John O'Neal
Simon O'Neal
Benjamine G. O'Neal
John Gaskill
Amasa Simpson
Wallace W. Simpson
William S. Tolson
John Williams
Francis Williams
Robert Williams

They risked their lives during peace and war in order to keep commerce moving through Ocracoke Inlet.

Ocracoke Inlet is the only inlet on the Outer Banks that remains at the same location, and has not filled in only to wash out again farther north or south of its original location. Hatteras Inlet has sanded up and washed out farther to the north three times. Drum Inlet to the south and Oregon Inlet farther north have also moved.

In 1797 Jonathan Price stated that Ocracoke still retained the name of an island though it was at that time a peninsula, a heap of sand having gradually filled up the space that divided it from the bank. He described Ocracoke Village:

> green trees that over strikingly distinguish it from the sandy beach to which it has been joined. The length is three miles, and its breadth two and one

PILOTS
(cont.)

1860 CENSUS
David Ballance
W.H. Ballance
Samuel Bragg
Josephus Fulcher
Josephus Fulcher, Jr.
Simon Garish
Andrew Jackson
Samuel Spencer
Thomas Jackson
Thomas O'Neal
Joseph O'Neal
Amasa Simpson
Jordan William
Bateman Scarborough
H.B. Williams

1870 CENSUS
William Ballance
Benjamine Gaskins
Amon Howard
Simon Howard
James Styron
Thomas Styron

1880 CENSUS
Joseph O'Neal

1900 CENSUS
James M.Bragg
Samuel D. Bragg

This 1795 survey map by Jonathan Price shows the shipping channel and one settlement each on Portsmouth Island, Beacon Island, and Shell Castle Island, and two settlements on Ocracoke Island. The one on the south end of the island I believe to be Pilot Town.

A study of maps of this area for the last two hundred years shows that the "hook" at the south point of Ocracoke Island has washed away and built back many times. Even so, the remnants of the hook still remain. The settlement near the hook is Pilot Town.

The area showing W.W. (William) Howard was the village near Cockle Creek (Silver Lake).

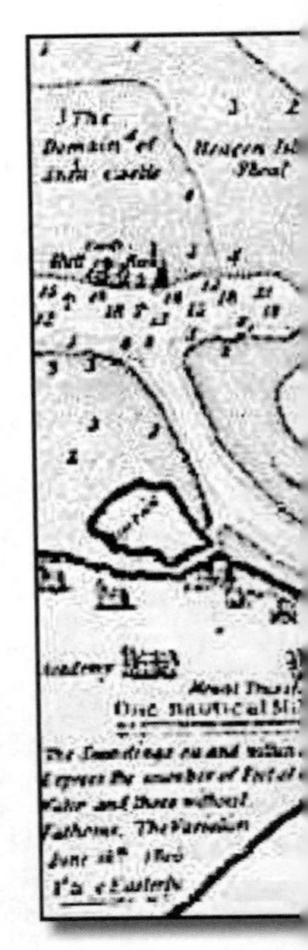

Map of Ocracoke Inlet (Price-Coles Survey, 1806)[1]
Upper left: Shell Castle, Old Fort-Beacon Island. Upper right: Ocracoke Island, Teaches Hole. Lower left: Portsmouth Island.

1 PUBLISHER'S NOTE: This map of "Ocracock Bar including Shell Castle," is said by some to be the work of Edmund M. Blunt, NY, 1809.

half miles. Small live oak and cedar grow abundantly over it and it contains several swamps and marshes which might be cultivated to great advantage, but its inhabitants depending on other elements for their support, suffer the earth to remain in its natural state. They are all Pilots and their number of head of family is about thirty.[3]

The government laid off fifty acres of land on Ocracoke for the use of the public. This land was to be used by the pilots to build huts to live in and to have a place to pull up their boats for paint and repair. The huts were but one or two rooms, some with dirt floors. Later, after William Howard bought the island and some of the pilots married into his family, he began to deed land over to them. They then built bigger houses.

The public land laid off for the pilots came to be known as Pilot Town. David Stick and others have suggested that

3 Jonathan Price, "A Description of Occacock Inlet," 1795

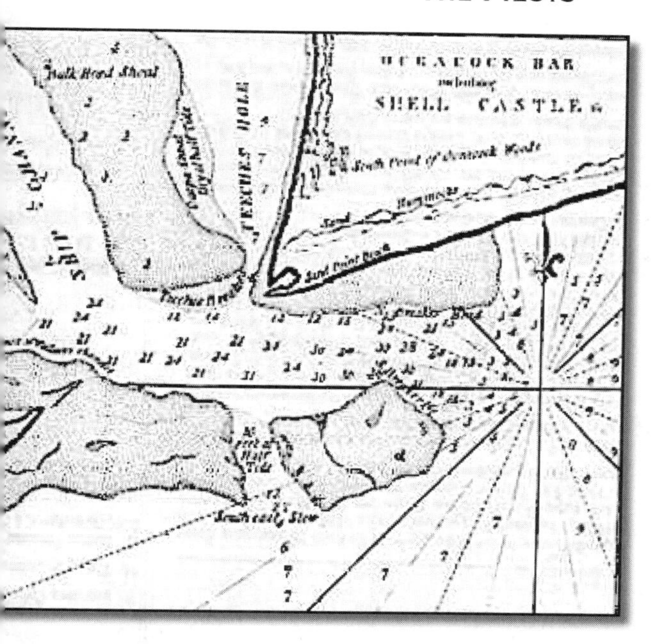

what was Pilot Town is now the village of Ocracoke.[4] From my research, I do not arrive at the same conclusion. First of all, Pilot Town had to be located at a spot where there was a clear view of the inlet. Ships wanting to take on a pilot would lie outside the inlet and raise a flag signaling need for a pilot. Ocracoke Inlet cannot be seen from the present village. Upon seeing a signal, a pilot would row out, board the ship, and bring it across the bar. It would have taken him most of the day to reach the vessel from the present village. Jonathan Price's map dated 1795[5] shows a settlement on the south point of the island that must have been Pilot Town at that time. Through the years there were several tracts of land laid off for the pilots' use on the island. Each new tract was needed because of the previous one's washing away. An example comes from Laws of *North Carolina-1766* (Chapter 8, p. 670):

4 David Stick, *The Outer Banks of North Carolina* (The University of North Carolina Press, 11958), p. 300.

5 Price, *Survey*, p.7.

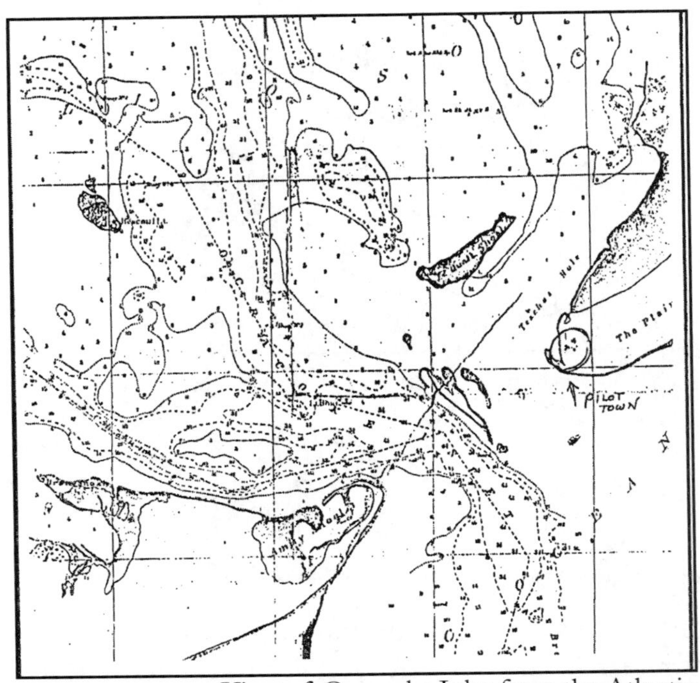

View of Ocracoke Inlet from the Atlantic Ocean. The small settlement on the south point of Ocracoke Island is believed to be the first Pilot Town, "which washed away." The map on the preceding page, dated 1806, does not show a settlement on the Ocracoke side of the inlet but does show the hook. The 1857 map above shows a settlement at the south end of Ocracoke and another located on the area now called Springer's Point. There could have been only one reason for a settlement on the point of the beach, that being for the convenience of the pilots. They built only small shacks because they knew they would wash away during storms and Pilot Town would change locations again. Those that married and stayed on the job built homes in the village for their families. The pilots stayed in the shacks when they were on duty.

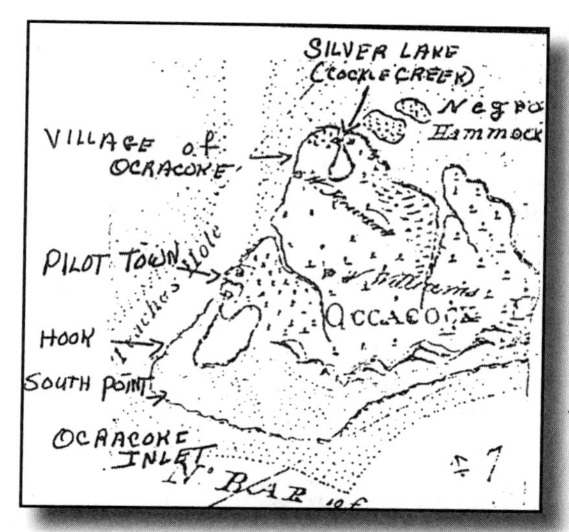

Close-up from Jonathan Price survey map on Page 85.

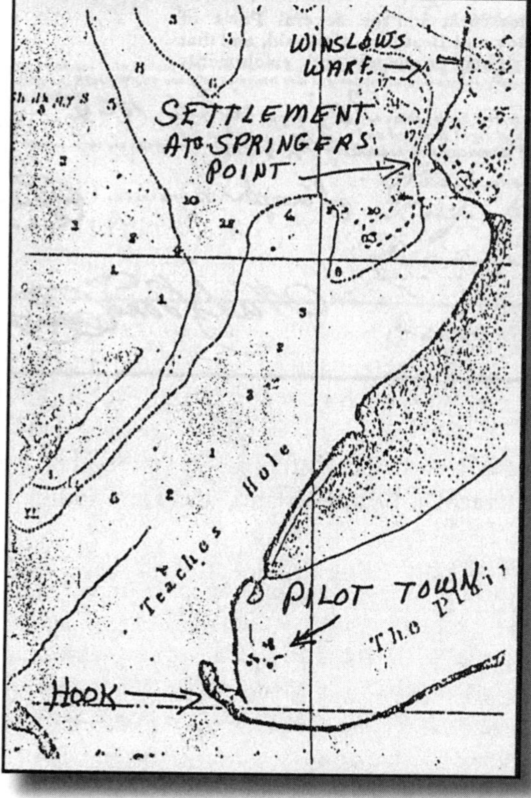

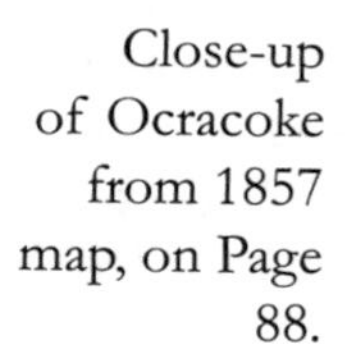
Close-up of Ocracoke from 1857 map, on Page 88.

These maps show that Pilot Town was not located in the village of Ocracoke.

> XVIII: And whereas the Pilots that attend Ocacock Bar, have petitioned this Assembly to have Privilege to build Houses and pull up their Boats on the Island of Ocacock, and the land formerly assigned for that Purpose being washed away,[6] and Disputes and Controversies concerning the Right of the Pilots to settle on said have arisen: Be it therefore Enacted by the Authority aforesaid, That any Three or more Commissioners appointed by this Act, shall attend at Ocacock Island within Six Months after the Passing of this Act, and lay off Twenty Acres of land in the most proper part of that Island, and value the same on Oath, and pay the Valuation-Money to the present Owners of Ocacock Island—to allot and lay of a part to every branch Pilot who may hereafter attend to Pilot and conduct vessels into Ocacock Inlet—during the term of residence, and no longer.

A Preliminary Survey of Ocracoke Inlet, dated 1857, shows a settlement on the southernmost point of Ocracoke Island at Ocracoke Inlet that I believe to have been another Pilot Town. In 1766, an "Act for Facilitating the Navigation of Port Bath, Port Roanoke, and Port Beaufort" was established and set forth the following regulations:

> Commissioners were appointed to contract with proper persons to examine, from time to time, the situation of the Swash and keep the channels leading from Ocracoke Bar, to Port Bath, Edenton and New Bern well and sufficiently staked out, and to erect Beacons at Ocracoke, Beacon Island, and Core Bank—for the safety of vessels.
>
> Said Commissioners shall have the authority to

6 In a letter dated May 10th, 1755, Arthur Dobbs Esq. Govr. writes from Portsmouth Island: "The Storms they tell me for some years past has made vast havoc among these sandy Islands, the opening of Ocacock Inlet enlarged from 2 miles to 4 miles wide." The two miles of beach that washed away could have been the original Pilot Town, since it would have been located as near the inlet as possible.

Pilot's Branch.

To all People to whom these Presents shall come..

KNOW Ye, That we John O. Blount Joseph [illegible] Nath Bond William Right [illegible] Bond Esquires, Commissioners of the Navigation of Port Roanoke, in the State of North-Carolina, having examined Christopher Oneal Jun touching his abilities as a Pilot, and it being also certified unto us that he is a good orderly and peaceable citizen of this State, and that he is a proper and well qualified person to be and act as a Pilot for the Bar of Occacock, and the several ports of Bath, Roanoke, Currituck, and Beaufort:

THESE *are therefore to make known,* That the said [illegible] is empowered to be and act as a Pilot for the Bar of Occacock, and the several Ports of Bath, Roanoke, Currituck and Beaufort, aforesaid, and that he is entitled to all the rights, privileges and emoluments thereunto belonging.

GIVEN under our Hands and Seals, this 30 *day of* July 1824. *one thousand eight hundred and* 24 *and in the* XVIII *year of American Independence.*

Joseph [illegible] (Seal)

W. Right Nath Bond

PILOT'S BRANCH.

To all People to whom these presents shall come:

Know ye—that we, Wallace W. Simpson Benjamin oneal Joseph Roberts Francis Williams Sen.

Esquires, Commissioners of Navigation for the Port of Ocracoke

in the State of North Carolina, having received from the Board of Branch Pilots, appointed by an act of the General Assembly, passed in the year of our Lord one thousand eight hundred and twenty-four, a certificate of Christopher oneal

being qualified to act as a Pilot for the Bar and Swashes, and he the said Christopher oneal

having satisfied us of his being qualified to Pilot in the sounds of Pamlico and Albemarle to the Ports of Edenton Elizabeth City and Plymouth:—These are to make known, that he said Christopher oneal

is empowered to be and act as a Pilot for the Bar of Ocracoke and the Swashes, and from thence to the Ports of Edenton, Elizabeth City and Plymouth; and that he is entitled to all the rights, privileges and emoluments thereunto belonging

Given under our hands and seals at Ocracoke March 22 1859

Wallace W Simpson (Seal)
Benja. G. Oneal (Seal)
Francis William (Seal)

Above: Pilot's license issued July 30, 1824, to Christopher O'Neal, Jr., great-great-great-grandfather of the author. Below: License issued March 22, 1859, to Christopher O'Neal, the author's great-great-grandfather.

AUTHOR COLLECTION

View of Ocracoke Inlet, from Pamlico Sound, during portions of the 1700s and 1800s.

DRAWING BY ELLEN FULCHER CLOUD

examine Pilots touching their qualifications. In order to obtain his warrant to Pilot Vessels in all or any ports—in case any person shall pretend to pilot or take charge of any vessel or ship without having passed an Examination and obtaind a warrant for so doing and also posted bond of One Hundred Pounds, with two good securities, And be it Enacted, that there shall be paid to every Pilot who shall take charge of any Ship or vessel, the following Pilotage: that is to say; For every ship or vessel from the outside of the Bar of Ocracoke into Beacon Island Road. Two Shillings, Proclamation Money, per Foot for every vessel that draws Nine feet of water, or less; and for every vessel drawing Ten Feet and upwards, Three Shillings per foot. And when any vessel whatsoever shall make a Signal for a Pilot or not, any Pilot who shall go over the Bar aforesaid to Pilot such vessel into Port, and offer his service for that purpose, shall be entitled, although the Master[7] of such ves-

7 *master*: captain of a ship.

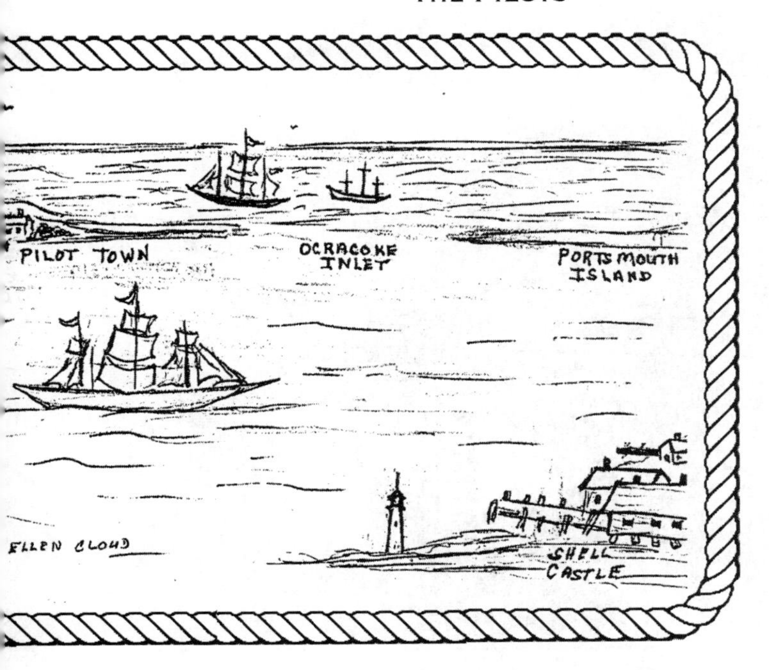

sel shall refuse to employ him, to half the fees which he would be in entitled to if he had taken charge, and piloted such vessel over the Bar, and the Master shall be obliged to pay the same.

In 1773 George Bell, John Bragg, Adam Gaskill,[8] Richard Wade, William Styron, and Simon Hall, all pilots at Ocracoke Inlet, sent a petition to the governor complaining that a number of black men, some of whom were slaves brought down by their owners, and also other freedmen of color were trying to take over their jobs and were seriously affecting their business.

This problem was soon taken care of, and the pilots continued to serve the needs of the shipping industry and to risk their lives protecting the coast during times of war.

8 This was Adam Gaskins. The name Gaskill and Gaskins were often confused in these old records.

An Ocracoke monument commemorates the earthen Fort Ocracoke, which was first destroyed by Confederates who left it to advancing Union forces, "which completed the destruction." The other side lists soldiers from Ocracoke and Portsmouth islands.

CHAPTER 8

War and Military Activites

THE AMERICAN REVOLUTION

Ocracoke Inlet played a vital part in shipping during the American Revolutionary War. British cruisers had closed the "Cape Feare and Chesapeak Bays" and were keeping a close watch at Beaufort. Merchants of New Bern, Washington, Edenton, and Bath sent vessels abroad with cargoes of tobacco and pork, and in return received powder, ammunition, salt, and clothing, which slipped in through Ocracoke Inlet. Some of this was then shipped across the shallow waters of Pamlico and Albemarle sounds to South Quay on the mainland, and then by wagon over land to

Washington's army at Valley Forge.[1]

The shoals at Ocracoke Bar were dangerous and almost impossible to cross without the aid of the pilots living at Ocracoke. The pilots were the first to come face to face with the enemy at the beginning of war, for one of the first goals of the enemy (whoever it may have been) was always to blockade the Ocracoke Inlet, thus threatening the business of piloting. The pilots were loyal to the colonies and eager to bring in ships favorable to the colonies and leave those favorable to the British outside the bar.

On April 14 the British ship *Lily* captured the vessel *Polly*. On the same day a privateer[2] recaptured the *Polly* and-disarmed the *Lily*. The pilots at Ocracoke lnlet showed their determination to keep the inlet open to shipping. In a period of three days a group of armed pilots manned five whale boats, proceeded out of the Inlet, captured both vessels, and took them to New Bern.

With the attempt to blockade the inlet came a decrease in the need for pilots. Though some were still active, others decided to go privateering. Still others joined the militia.

Because of the immediate danger to shipping and protection for the coast, a fort was built on Beacon Island.[3] A battery was placed at Ocracoke. The *Caswell*, with 145 men commanded by Willis Williams, was stationed at the Bar. On July 12, 1776, Capt. James Anderson wrote to the Council of Safety: "I have made up my Company at Ocracoke—I hope to be capable of guarding against all enemies who may offer to oppose us here." On July 27, 1776, the commissioners approved the sum of two hundred pounds to be

---

1 *The Story of Ocracoke Island*, A Hyde County Bicentennial Project.

2 ***privateers***: vessels owned and operated by local seaman, carrying papers from the government authorizing them to capture merchant vessels of the enemy, then sell the cargo and ship or keep the ship for themselves.

3 See map, page 86.

paid to Capt. James Anderson "for the purpose of procuring goods and sufficient Guns, drums, and Colours for the use of his Independent Company on the sea coast in this colony." Anderson also was furnished fifty weight of gun powder and one hundred weight of lead.[4]

Virginia also knew of the importance of Ocracoke Inlet and agreed to construct two row galleys[5] for North Carolina for the purpose of protecting the inlet. North Carolina had no navy but began to convert small two-masted brigs into warships. There was a joint effort proposed between Virginia and North Carolina to protect the inlet. Virginia was to build the row galleys and North Carolina was to fit them out.

The *Caswell* took station at Ocracoke Inlet in the spring of 1778. The other row galley that was to join the *Caswell* at Ocracoke was the *Washington*. Having these vessels on station in the inlet did not by any means solve the problems there, for it was next to impossible to find crew members. Most men on the Outer Banks had already joined the militia or were privateering. Wages on the privateers were twice that of the Continental or state navies, and the chances to obtain prize money were much greater on the privateers.

The *Caswell* remained at its station but took little or no part in protecting the inlet. The captain left the ship to travel to New Bern to request leave to visit his family, saying that there was no activity at the inlet. Meanwhile, the pilots and privateers continued to capture ships and supplies. The *Caswell* lay idle until she was worm eaten, and she sank two years after her construction.

A petition was sent to Governor Caswell. It requested that the men of the Outer Banks be excused from the draft as they were constantly called upon to defend the coast

---

4 *Colonial Records*, Vol. VII, p. 687.

5 ***galley***: a long, low, usually single-decked ship propelled by oars and sails.

against British marauders.

The names of the men who served in Captain Anderson's Company have not been found. There is no way of knowing how many of them were Ocracoke pilots. One thing is certain. Every man on the island played a big part in the protection of the country during this war.

Twenty-two years later, when the first census was taken, there were only forty-seven free white males living on Ocracoke Island. Judging by the rate of increase in population during the subsequent twenty years, there were probably fewer than thirty males living here in 1778. Of that number, probably twenty-five were in the militia, several were pilots, and at least three enlisted in the Continental Line at Halifax.

The following comes from a list of men in the *Troop Returns, 1770-1778*, North Department of Archives and History.

AGE	NAME	ABODE	BORN	HEIGHT	HAIR	EYES
18	Chris Neale (O'Neal)	Ocracoke	Hatteras	5'6"	brown	dark
16	Francis Neale (O'Neal)	Ocracoke	Hatteras	5'6"	light	grey
20	Thomas Neale (O'Neal)	Ocracoke	Hatteras	5'6"	light	grey

THE WAR OF 1812

On June 18, 1812, the House and Senate of the United States Congress passed a resolution declaring "that War be and the same is hereby declared to exist between the United Kingdom of Great Britain and Ireland and the dependencies thereof and the United States of America and their territories."[6]

For several years, the various European countries had been at war with one another. The United States wished to remain neutral in order to trade with all western countries. England began to seize American ships on the high seas to prevent supplies getting to their enemies. England also seized sailors off the ships in order to man her war vessels. This was the major reason for America's declaration of war. The president had placed an embargo on American ships to keep them at home. This act was resented by the merchants and they refused to obey it. Seizure of American ships continued, and war was finally declared against the western nations who had "long since been waging war against the United States."[7]

Shortly after war was declared, North Carolina found that she was on her own as far as financing her troops and supplies. Many troops served their time without ever being paid and went home without any money when they were released.[8]

The state had to finance its entire involvement in the war and was not reimbursed until a hundred years later, in 1916, when the United States Congress recommended that North Carolina be reimbursed.[9]

The North Carolina coast was not armed or protected in any way, even though most of this war took place at sea. North Carolina contributed both to the United States Navy and to privateering.

In eastern North Carolina privateering came to be a big business in which local seamen participated. The priva-

---

6 *North Carolina and the War of 1812*, by Sarah McCulloh Lemmon.

7 *Ibid.*

8 *Ibid.*

9 *Ibid.*

teers tried to capture merchant vessels of the enemy, and sell the cargo and ships or keep the ships for themselves. In peacetime they would have been considered pirates, but in time of war they were licensed by the government. The privateers' boats ran from small schooners to large, three-masted, heavily armed vessels. Altogether, 526 American privateers captured or destroyed 1,334 British merchantmen during the course of the war.[10]

Even though many Ocracoke men were privateers, the coast remained unguarded. Among the John Gray Blount Papers, Department of Archives and History, is the following letter to Gov. William Hawkins, dated May 25, 1813.

> Dear Sir
>
> An express Boat which left Ocacok Bar this morning informs that on Friday last a Schooner with American Colours anchored off the Barr on which a Pilot Boat with four Hands went on board & were informed that the Schooner wanted to come in over the Bar. & still pretended to be Americans & were very liberal in their abuse of the Brltish, but in a short time informed the Pilots that she was the Bntish Schooner the *Venus* late the Highflying Privateer of Baltimore and that she must be piloted in over the Bar. On the Pilots assuring them there was not water sufficient for her draft to come in safely they man'd the Pilot Boat with the avowed intention of burning the Revenue Cutter and other Vessels then within the Bar and left the schooner with the signal for a Pilot still flying. In proceeding in to execute their truly British plan they met another Pilot Boat going out to the schooner which they ordered along side of them, and inform'd them they were in want of water on board & requested that they would proceed on board and take on shore a few Casks to fill for them no doubt supposing they would proceed onboard and be detained, but they observing the number of armed men and the silence of their Brother Pilots in the first Boat,

10 *Ibid.*

supposed that all was not right & proceeded no farther towards the schooner than to get off the mark of their muskets & then rowed on shore and give the alarm. On the Officer on the boat observing that, he observed that he wish he had sunk that Boat, that they now must return as she would give the Alarm. They did return on board & in a short time discharged the Pilots observing that they would soon return better prepared to execute their design, & on Sunday last they again return'd off the Bar & took a Sloop which had just gone out.

Letters by this boat inform that the Revenue Cutter was not maned or prepared in any way to make residence & that few Inhabitants on both sides of the Inlet are without arms or ammunition but are well disposed not only to resist the attack of the British but to render every assistance to the shipping within the Bar, which are now left wholly unprotected by the sending away the two Gun Boats which were stationed there.

From having understood that you intended sending two Companies of Milita to each of the Towns of Edenton, Washington, New Bern and Wilmington, I have taken the liberty of giving you the information this day received and beg leave to offer it is my opinion that one company stationed Ocacock composed of men accustomed to the water and commanded by a brave and enterprising Captain also acquainted with Ocacock & their Pilot Boats to assist & Supply the Inhabitants there with Arms & Ammunition would afford more security to all the Northern parts on North Carolina as well as the numerous Vessels now daily arriving there from the Blockade of Virginia. Ball procured there will be nothing to fear from insurrection and if one Company selected from Hyde or some of the counties accustomed to the water & commanded by the most active & popular Pilot on Ocacock Island and the US Government can be prevailed on to order back to Ocacock the two Gun Boats lately ordered from there, there will be little danger at Ocacock And without that or the building a Fort on Beacon Island, There is no safety for vessels or other property at Ocacock or its vicinity or even in the Towns of New Bern, Washington or Edenton. The importance of the Subject to myself & my fellow Citizens will I hope justify me in liberty I have in writing you thus freely

I am with much respect
your Excellency most Obedt
Sem. JGBlount

On July 11, 1813, before Governor Hawkins could reply, a British fleet of nine ships, nineteen barges, and two thousand men anchored off Ocracoke. On July 12, they made their attack on unarmed Ocracoke and Portsmouth, seizing two hundred cattle, four hundred sheep, and sixteen hundred fowl. They broke up all the furniture in the houses, ripped open beds, threw feathers to the wind, and robbed women and children of their clothes.

After the attack, Col. Nathan Tisdale called out the New Bern militia and sent an urgent message for help to Governor Hawkins. Gov. William Hawkins' reply to Blount came on July 23, 1813. It was an apology for his delay and stated that he was strongly "in favor of erecting a fortification on Beacon Island . . . I shall go to Ocracoke perhaps tomorrow for the purpose of satisfying myself by actual observation as to the property and practicability of building a fort on Beacon Island. ..."

On September 26, 1813, a pilot boat with four pilots aboard went to a little schooner that sat off the bar, thinking she was waiting for a pilot. The crew was British. They took one of the pilots and the boat and made the other three men jump overboard into the breakers. When one refused he was pushed overboard. They then sent men ashore at Ocracoke with a white flag to announce officially that Ocracoke and Portsmouth were in a state of blockade. They seized a schooner while there and sent it to Nova Scotia to be sold.

Even with the blockade, the American privateers

manned with a crew of *Old Salts* from these Outer Banks managed to get through the blockade with the needed supplies.

These are just some close encounters that were written about in letters to the government. There is no way to estimate the number of such cases that were not recorded anywhere.

Nowhere in the history books do you find the names of these men. Occasionally a pilot is named in a letter written by a ship's captain. This is rare and inaccessible to the general public. (See pages 82-84 for names of the Ocracoke pilots.)

THE CIVIL WAR

The Civil War was very short lived on the Outer Banks. North Carolina seceded from the Union on May 20, 1861. On August 29, 1861, Fort Hatteras was captured by Federal troops. Shortly afterwards, they took control of all of the Outer Banks, blocking entrance to Pamlico Sound as well as the Albemarle.

The local men fought with the Confederate States Army, also for a very short time. They were not employed in protecting the coast during this war. Records were found of only one local resident serving with the Confederate States Navy, Christopher O'Neal,[11] a pilot, transferred from the 33rd Regiment to the Navy on April 3, 1864.

On March 14, 1862, the Union troops took New Bern after winning a fierce battle in which most of our Ocracoke soldiers took part. It was on this date that all local men with

11 Author's great-great grandfather

Company H deserted or left the 33rd Regiment, with which they were serving. Their first lieutenant, Wilson Tilmon Farrow, also of Ocracoke, resigned on the same day. This raises a question: Did he resign because all the local men deserted or did all the local men leave because he resigned? Records do not show the answer.

The Outer Bankers did not feel that this was their war, and wanted very little to do with it. Other than dismantling the lighthouse (which was done by the Confederates), the only recorded damage at Ocracoke was the burning of two schools and a few homes. The Federal troops who made a quick survey of Ocracoke Island after the capture of Hatteras are credited with this destruction.

By mid-1862 the Union had control of the coastal sound counties and New Bern was their headquarters.

North Carolina had more deaths in battle than any other Confederate state. Some forty thousand North Carolina soldiers died from battle wounds or diseases contracted from the living conditions in both camp and battlefield, from malnutrition, and from neglect.

The troops saw their friends die at their sides, leaving widows and children with no means of support. North Carolina troops began to desert in large numbers. There were more than twenty-three thousand deserters, some of whom returned to duty after they found it impossible to reach home or after they had visited home and found the family in satisfactory condition. From microfilm of old newspapers published in Washington, North Carolina, 1807-1881, comes the following description of the inlets on the North Carolina coast.

The New York Times
Thursday, Sept. 5, 1861

External Commerce of the sounds is dependant on three inlets, Hatteras, Ocracoke, and Old Topsail. [now

Beaufort Inlet]. There is another Inlet called New Inlet or Oregon Inlet which according to U.S. Coast Survey, is almost worthless for navigation. Hatteras Inlet easily admits vessels drawing 15 ft. of water. Ocracoke in mean low water, admits over it's bar vessels drawing 10 ft. to 11 ft. It's defences are believed to be insegnificant even compared with those at Hatteras. Old Topsail Inlet at Beaufort, is said to be the best on the North Carolina coast. It is defended by Fort Macon, and, the rebels say, in a very efficient manner. But so they thought of Hatteras. There is but one other Harbor of importance on all the Coast of North Carolina, that of Wilmington—the roads of the Cape Fear River, which empties into the Atlantic 50 or 60 miles down the coast from Beaufort. The navigation of the sounds down to Beaufort is tortuous and tedious and not at all reliable or safe. The closing of Hatteras Inlet therefor inflicts a heavy blow on all the contraband, Commerce and Privateering enterprise in which Virginia and North Carolina have been indulging. Fort Hatteras is made a naval depot for our blockading fleet, and it is easy see that a reasonable force within it, and a war vessel nearby to beat off landing parties, will make the position imprignable to the enemy.

We shall not wait long, we hope to hear that Ocracoke Inlet and Fort Macon are under our control.

The following information comes from NCST, Moore's Roster, Vol. 2. Note the number of enlistments on October 17, 1861, and the number of desertions on March 14, 1862.

Ocracoke Soldiers of Company H, 33rd Regiment

BALANCE, HOLLOWAY, Private
Resided in Hyde County, enlisted Oct. 17 1861. Present

and accounted for until ***March 14, 1862, when he was reported absent without leave.*** Dropped from the rolls of company. Reenlisted in company Sept. 20, 1863. Present and accounted for until Captured at or near Gravel Hill Va., about July 28, 1864. Confined at Point Lookout, Md., Aug. 5, 1864. Transferred to Elmira, N.Y., on Aug. 8, 1864. Died at Elmira on Nov. 7, 1864, of "pneumonia."

BALLANCE, WILLIAM R., Private
Resided in Hyde County, enlisted Oct. 17, 1861. Mustered in as private. Present or accounted for until *captured at New Bern on March 14, 1862.* Exchanged at Aikens Landing, James River, Va., Aug. 5, 1862. Returned to duty prior to Nov. 1, 1862. Present or accounted for until wounded in the right arm at Gettysburg, Pa., July 3, 1863. Returned to duty in Sept.-Oct. 1863. Promoted to corporal on March 1, 1864. Reduced to ranks on Dec. 15, 1864; present or accounted for until he deserted to the enemy on or about Feb. 24, 1865. Confined at Washington, D.C., Feb. 27, 1865. Released on an unspecified date after taking the Oath of Allegiance.

BRAGG WILLIAM B., Private
Resided in Hyde County, where he enlisted Oct. 17, 1861. Present or accounted for until *March 14, 1862, when he was reported absent without leave.*

FARROW, ISAAC LITTLETON, 1st Lieutenant
Resided in Hyde County, where he enlisted on Oct. 17, 1861. Mustered in as 1st sergeant, appointed 3rd lieutenant on Dec. 25, 1862, and transferred to Co. I of this regiment; promoted to lst lieutenant Aug. l, 1863, and transferred back to this company present and accounted for until killed at Wilderness, Va., on or about May 5, 1864. He was "a brave and gallant Soldier." He was "Always at the Port of Duty."

FARROW WILSON TILMON, 1st Lieutenant
Resided in Hyde County, appointed 1st lieutenant on Oct

16, 1861. Present or accounted for until he *resigned March 14, 1862*. Reason he resigned not reported.

FULCHER, JOSEPHUS, Corporal
Resided in Hyde County, enlisted Oct. 17, 1861, mustered in as corporal. Present or accounted for until *March 14, 1862, when he was reported absent without leave*. Dropped from the rolls of the company prior to Nov. 1, 1862.

GARRISH, BENJAMINE J., Private
Resided in Forsyth County and enlisted in Hyde County at age 17 on Oct 17, 1861. Present or accounted for until wounded in the left thigh at Grimes Mill, Va., June 27, 1862. Reported absent without leave in Nov.-Dec. 1862. Failed to retum to duty and was dropped from the rolls of the company in March-April 1864.

GASKILL, WILLIAM, Sergeant
Resided in Hyde County where he enlisted on Oct. 17, 1861. Mustered in as sergeant. Present or accounted for until killed at Cedar Mountain, Va., Aug. 9, 1862.

GASKINS, GEORGE, Private
Resided in Forsyth County and enlisted in Hyde County on Oct.17, 1861. Presented and accounted for until he deserted on or about Jan. 22, 1862.

HOWARD, AMBROSE J., Private
Resided in Hyde County, enlisted at age 33 on Oct. 17, 1861. Present and accounted for through April 1862. No further records. (N.C. pension records indicate that he survived the war.)

HOWARD, ROBERT, Private
Resided in Hyde County, where he enlisted on Oct. 17, 1861. Present or accounted for until *March 14, 1862, when he was reported absent without leave.*

JACKSON, GEORGE W., 1st Sergeant
Resided in Hyde County, enlisted on Oct 17, 1861. Mustered in as private. Promoted to corporal in Jan.-Feb. 1863. Promoted to sergeant in March-April 1863. Wounded in the right thigh and captured at Chancellorsville, Va., May 3, 1863. Hospitalized at Washington, D.C. Paroled at Old Capital Prison, Washington, June 25, 1863, and transferred to City Point, Va., where he was received on June 30, 1863, for exchange. Returned to duty in Sept.-Oct. 1863. Promoted to 1st sergeant on Nov. l, 1863. Present or accounted for until killed at Wilderness, Va., May 6, 1864.

JACKSON, HENDERSON F., Private
Resided in Hyde County, enlisted Oct. 7, 1861. Present or accounted for until he deserted on or about Jan. 22, 1862, and "jointed the enemy."

O'NEAL, BENJAMINE, Private
Resided in Hyde County, enlisted Oct. 17, 1861. Present or accounted for until captured near Greenville on Nov. 24-25, 1863. Confined at Point Lookout, Md., Dec. 29, 1863; paroled and transferred to City Point, Va., where he was received on April 30, 1864, for exchange. Returned to duty.

O'NEAL, CHRISTOPHER JR., Private[12]
Resided in Hyde County, enlisted age 44 on Oct. 17, 1861. Present or accounted for until *March 14, 1862, when he was reported absent without leave.* Re-turned to duty in March 1863. Present or accounted for until transferred to Confederate States Navy on or about April 3, 1864.

Christopher O'Neal, Jr.
AUTHOR COLLECTION

12 Author's great, great grandfather

O'NEAL, FRANCIS W., Private
Resided in Hyde County, where he enlisted on Oct. 17, 1861. Present or accounted for until he was reported *missing on March 14, 1862.*

O'NEAL, SIMON H., Private
Resided in Hyde County where he enlisted on Oct. 17, 1861. Present or accounted for until *March 14, 1862, when he was reported absent without leave.* Returned to duty in Sept.-Oct. 1863. Present or accounted for until he deserted to the enemy on or about Feb. 24, 1865. Confined at Washington, D.C., Feb. 27, 1865. Released on an unspecified date after taking the Oath of Allegiance.

SPENCER, ANDREW S., Private
Resided in Hyde County, enlisted Dec. 8, 1861, present or accounted for until April 1862. Dropped from rolls prior to Nov. 1, 1862, "for long absence."

STYRON, ELIJAH, Private
Enlisted in Hyde County, age 30, on Oct. 17, 1861. Present or accounted for until *March 14, 1862, when he was reported absent without leave.*

WILLIAMS, TILMOND FARROW, Private
Resided in Hyde County, enlisted at age 16 on Oct. 17, 1864. Mustered in as private. Captured at New Bern March 14, 1862. Received at Aikens Landing, James River, Va., July 12, 1862, for exchange. Declared exchanged at Aikens Landing on Aug. 5, 1862. Reported absent in hospital through Oct. 1862. Returned to duty Nov.-Dec. 1862. Present or accounted for until wounded in thigh and hip at Chancellorsville, Va., May 3, 1863. Promoted to sergeant Sept.-Oct 1863.Promoted to 1st sergeant July 22, 1864. Reduced in ranks on Dec. 15, 1864, by sentence of court-martial. Reason he was court martialled not reported. Deserted to the enemy on or about Feb. 24, 1865. Confined at Washington, D.C., Feb. 27, 1865. Released on an unspecified date after taking the Oath of Allegiance.

Fort Ocracoke in the Civil War[1]

On March 20th, 1861, the same day that North Carolina seceded from the Union, the Washington Grays, along with a procession of steamers and schooners, were sent to Beacon Island, bringing building materials, arms, and supplies. The troops immediately began construction of the fort and, despite the hardships involved, had it almost completed when Brigadier General Gwynn visited 10 days later. The general reported to Governor John Willis Ellis that the fort had five guns mounted and twelve more to be mounted within the next few days.

The following troops were mustered into the State Ser-

View of Ocracoke Inlet from Fort Ocracoke on Beacon Isl

DRAWING BY ELLEN FULCHER CL

"Destruction of Fort Ocracoke on Beacon Island, at the entrance of Pamlico Sound, Sept. 17, 1861, by an expedition under command of Lieut. Eastman, of the 'Pawnee'."

DRAWING, THE NEW YORK ILLUSTRATED NEWS, OCT. 7, 1861

vice at Fort Ocracoke on July 13, 1861: the Tar River Boys and the Hertford Light Infantry. Mustered into service at Beacon Island on June 20, 1861, were the Morrison Guards and the Confederate Guards from Washington County.

When the bombardment of the forts at Hatteras began, most of these troops were sent to Hatteras to help protect the forts, and were captured at the fall of Fort Hatteras on Aug. 29, 1861. Those that remained at Fort Ocracoke abandoned the fort upon learning that Fort Hatteras had been captured. The fort had not received all requested supplies and the skeleton of troops left at the fort was not sufficient to secure the fort from the enemy.

—

1 PUBLISHER'S NOTE: This story is excerpted from a piece the author wrote after the publication of ***Old Salt***.

(North Carolina pension records indicate he was shot in the right thigh and left heel as a result of the explosion of a shell; he suffered a fractured skull and his left eye was "almost destroyed" at Chancellorsville.)

Ocracoke Soldiers of Company F, 33rd Regiment

O'NEAL, JOHN, Private
Resided in Hyde County, where he enlisted Sept. 9, 1861. Present or accounted for until he died in Hospital at Gordonsville, Va., May 29, 1862, of pneumonia.

O'NEAL, JOHN M., Private
Resided in Hyde County, enlisted Sept. 9, 1861. Present or accounted for until wounded in the right thigh and right thumb at Fredericksburg , Va., Dec. 13, 1862. Right thumb amputated. Reported absent, wounded, through Dec. 1862. Deserted Jan. 1863. Listed as a deserter through Feb. 1864. Reported absent on furlough May-June 1864. Reported absent sick, during July-Oct. 1864. Returned to duty in Nov.-Dec. 1864. Present or accounted for until paroled at Lynchburg, Va., April 13-15, 1865.

O'NEAL, WILLIAM W., Private.
Resided in Hyde County where he enlisted on Sept.9, 1861. Present or accounted for until he died at Winchester, Va., Oct. 12, 1862, cause of death not reported.

Ocracoke Soldiers with Company B, 17th Regiment

DAILY, FABIUS F., private, enlisted May 1 , 1862, Hyde County; Co. B, 17th Regt.

GASKILL, WILLIAM B., private, enlisted May 1, 1862, Hyde County; Co. B, 17th Regt.

GASKINS, C.S., private, enlisted May 1, 1862, Hyde

County; Co. B., 17th Regt.

WAHAB, JAMES H., enlisted May 1, 1862, promoted corporal June 17, 1862; Co. B., 17th Regt.

Company M, 19th Regiment

WAHAB, DALLAS, corporal, resided Hyde County, enlisted Fauquier County, Va., Nov. 1, 1862, mustered in a private, appointed corporal Aug. 1864. Present or accounted for through September 1864. Captured on Southside Railroad, west of Newport News, Va., April 6, 1865, and confined at Newport News, Va., until released after taking the oath of Allegiance June 30, 1865.

It is evident that the seafaring men of Ocracoke played little if any part in protecting the coast in this war.[13] After the Civil War, shipping through Ocracoke Inlet was on a steady decrease. The census records showing the occupation of "pilot" clearly indicate this fact.

13 More information on Civil War activities by other troops at Ocracoke Inlet, Beacon Island, and Portsmouth Island can be found in *Portsmouth: The Way It Was.*

Portion of image depicting ship at nearby Shell Castle Island in the late 1700s/early 1800s, printed on a pitcher.

NORTH CAROLINA MUSEUM OF HISTORY

CHAPTER 9

Ship Building

When shipping through Ocracoke Inlet became so great, many residents of the island began to ship out on the vessels, some as masters and some as crewmen. Many men had already sailed halfway around the world by the age of twenty.

Soon they purchased ships of their own. Many had ships built right here on Ocracoke. Ship building became a main source of income for some residents. Custom records show that many ships were built here. Only one record has been found that indicates the name of the very earliest ship-builder. In the estate papers of one Simon H. Garrish is a record of his personal belongings. The inventory lists tools of a ship builder. No other items are listed, not even household items, which leads one to believe he must have been living in someone else's home at the time of his death.

Certificates of enrollments at Ocracoke, 1815-1866, list ten ships built at Ocracoke between the years of 1824 and 1847, ranging from thirty-nine feet to seventy-two feet in length. Some had figureheads. Three of these vessels were owned in part by Simon H. Garrish.

One need only inspect the few remains of the many shipwrecks scattered on the beach at Ocracoke to realize

Inventory and Acct. of Sales of the Chattle Property of Simon H. Garrish, decd. made by his Administrator, Amasa Simpson, on the 28th day March 1848.

Article Sold	Purchaser	$	Cts
1 lot of 2 plains	Robert Gaskins	1	60
1 lot of 2 plains	John Pike	1	00
1 lot of 3 plains	Tilmon Farrow	1	55
1 lot of 2 plains	Tilmon Farrow	2	00
1 lot of 3 plain irons	John Pike		75
1 square & compass	Tilmon Farrow		40
1 handsaw	Amasa Simpson		45
1 __?__saw	Thomos Bragg		91
2 hammers	Tilmon Farrow		50
1 lot of 4 chisels	Thomas Bragg		67
1 lot of 3 rasp	William H. Howard		25
1 lot-2 pl-?- & fid&c	Tilmon Farrow		36
1 core sale needles	Tilmon Farrow		30
1 carpenters Adzr	Robert Gaskins	1	30
1 carpenters Ax	Robert Gaskins	1	80
1 lot of 5 Augers	Tilmon Farrow	1	15
2 pair dividers	Wm. Ballance		06
1 lot of files & sanders	Thomas Bragg		25
Brace and Bit	Tilmon Farrow	1	50
1 lot of 5 grindbelts?	Thomas Bragg		26
1 gun	Amasa Simpson		50
1 lot lumber-2 pieces	Wm. H. Howard		52
1 lot lumber	Euphemi Curtis	4	77
		$22	75

the craftsmanship and tools used in the master building of a vessel. They were all hand sawed or chopped with an axe. Traditionally the ship's carpenter also carved the figurehead that was placed on the bow of the vessels. One can only visualize figureheads used.

Later boat builders (mid- to late 1800s) were Jobe Wahab, Tilmon Farrow, and Josephus Fulcher (census records).

The information on the facing page was taken from the original Estate papers of Simon H. Garrish, found in the North Carolina Department of Archives and History in Raleigh, North Carolina.

It is reasonable to assume from old records that ships were built in the area now known as Springer's Point. The area near Teach's is the only place where there was water deep enough to launch such vessels. An old photograph of the area shows activities on the shore that appear to be related to ship building. The only records found on the subject of ship building are the custom records. These records tell the size of the vessels, the name, owners, masters, date built, place built, date surrendered, and reason surrendered.

OCRACOKE VESSELS[1]

Listed here are some of the records that relate to vessels owned or built at Ocracoke.

There are also some enrollments of other ports listed because either the owner or master was known to be a resident of Ocracoke.

1 PUBLISHER'S NOTE: This listing of vessels originally constituted a separate chapter in *Old Salt*.

Certificates of Enrollments at Ocracoke
1815, 1837 *1839, 1861* *1865, 1866*

Vessel Name

Sally Ann Owner: Richard Winslow, Ocracoke; George Jackson, master; built in Blackbow, Del., in 1817, enrolled Ocracoke July 1820; 1 deck, 1 mast, 55 ft. long, 19 ft. wide, 60 ton, square stern; Sloop.

Thomas Haggort Owners: William Howard & John Howard of Ocracoke; built in state of Conn. 1815; 1 deck, 2 mast, 56 ft. long, 18 ft. wide, 6 ft. deep, 46 ton, square stern; Schooner.

Lodge Owners: William Scarborough & Joseph Williams of Ocracoke; Joseph Williams, master; property change, 1824; 39 ft. long, 13 ft. wide, 4 ft. deep; Schooner.

Sidney Owners: George Howard, Simon B. Howard, & Cornelious Howard all of Ocracoke; built in Currituck in 1807; 1deck, 2 mast, 46 ft. long.

Henry Bateman Owners: Bateman O'Neal & James C. Garrish of Ocracoke; James C. Garrish, master; built at Ocracoke in 1826; 2 deck, 1 mast, 48 ft. long, 16 ft. wide, 4 ft. deep, 30 ton, square stern, no figurehead; enrolled 1827; Sloop.

Maner Owners: Thomas Bragg of Ocracoke & Banaster Ballance of Cape Hatteras; Banaster Ballance, master; built in Carteret Co. in 1819; 1 deck, 2 mast, 48 ft. long; Schooner.

Thomas H. Blount Owners: William Williams, Joseph Williams, George Hobbs & Simon Garrish; Joseph Williams, master; built in Currituck Co. in 1817; 1 deck, 2 mast, 45 ft. long, 15 ft. wide, 4ft. deep; enrolled Ocracoke 1828; Schooner.

(unknown) Owners: Jacob Gaskill & Richard _?_ of Ocracoke; Ivey Toler, master; 52 ft. long, April 1830; Schooner-June 1830, Benjamine Williams was

Master.

Henry Bateman Owners: Bateman O'Neal of Ocracoke and Richard Winslow, formerly of Ocracoke, but now about to remove to some other place; built at Ocracoke in 1826; Bateman O'Neal, master; 48 ft. long, 1 deck, 2 mast; July 1830.

Ind-, Owners: William Howard & Elisha Chase; William Howard, master; built Ocracoke in 1826; 1 deck, 1 mast, 45 ft. long, 14 ft. wide, 4 ft. 6 in. deep, 24 ton, square stern; enrolled 1833; Schooner.

-Vacate Owner: Comfort Dixon of Portsmouth; built in Straits in 1822; 48 ft. long, 13 ft. wide, 3ft. deep; enrolled 1833.

George Washington Owner: Elisha Chase; Joseph Jackson, master; built at Ocracoke 1824; 57 ft. long, 13 ft. wide, 3 ft. deep, 48 ton, 1 deck, 2 mast; possession change in part, 1833.

Brothers & Sisters Owner: Ann Howard, of Ocracoke; Thomas J. Heggaet, master; vessel was lengthened and rebuilt at Ocracoke, recorded Oct 1824; 48 ft long, 12 ft. wide, 4 ft. deep, 21 ton; now changed enrollment because of death of John Howard, 1833.

Levant Owner: William Howard; Francis Jackson, master; built on Pamlico Sound, near Cedar Hammack in Hyde Co. in 1829; 1 deck, l mast, 44 ft. long, 16 ft. wide, 5 ft. deep; square stern, billet head; ownership part change, 1833; Sloop

Young Eagle Owners: Thomas Bragg of Ocracoke and David Irerdell or (Tredswell) of Charleston SC; built in Carteret Co. 1830; property and district changed 1833.

Louis Ann Owners: Christopher O'Neal & Holloway Ballance of Ocracoke; Holloway Ballance, master; built in Hyde Co. 1828; reg. at Washington 1829;

44 ft. long, 15 ft. wide, 5 ft. deep, 30 ton; district and property change; reg. Ocracoke 1834; Schooner.

Spartan Owners: John Pike & William Howard; John Pike, master; built in Plymouth Mass. in 1825; 1 deck, 2 mast, 62 ft. long, 19ft. wide, 6ft. deep; 5087 ton; vessel condemned and sold at public auction; enrolled Ocracoke 1834; Schooner

Convoy Owners: Samuel Dudley, Wallis Styron & Thomas W. Styron, all of Portsmouth; Wallace Styron, master; built Skybrook, Conn. 1832; 1 deck, 2 mast, 65 ft. long, 21 ft. wide, 10ft. deep, 75 ton, square stern, Schroll head; change of property and district, reg. Ocracoke 1835; Schooner

Melissa Owner: Samuel Dudley; built Currituck Court House in 1829; district and property change, 1835; Schooner.

Hope Owners: Ira C. Gaskins & Robert Gaskins of Ocracoke; Ira Gaskins, master; built Currituck 1818; 1deck, 2 mast, 42 ft. long, 12 ft. wide, 4 ft. deep; enrolled Ocracoke 1836.

Brothers & Sisters Owners: Thomas D. Blackwell of Ocracoke & J.V. Blackwell of Medelleton, Hyde Co.; built Ocracoke; enrolled 1836; Schooner.

Henry Bateman Owner: George Hobbs of Ocracoke; Hobbs, master; built Ocracoke 1826; property change, 1836.

Wm. R. Smith Owners: Samuel Dudley of Portsmouth & Russel of New Bern; 1 deck, 2 mast, 67 ft. long, 17 ft. wide, 5ft. deep, 51 ton, square stern, billet head; 1837.

Paramount Owners: Wallace H. Styron & Simon H. Garrish; Wallace H. Styron, master; built at Ocracoke 1839; 1 deck, 2 mast, 52 ft., 17 ft. wide, 4 ft. deep, 36 ton; enrolled 29 Nov. 1839; Schooner.

Select Owner: Holloway Ballance; H. Ballance, master; built Currituck 1833; enrolled Ocracoke 1839; Schooner

Lafayett Owner: Ira C. Gaskins; Ira C. Gaskins, master; built New Jersey 1834; changed in property district, and from sloop to schooner; 1 deck, 2 mast, 55 ft. long, 18 ft. wide, 4 ft. deep; 1839.

Laura Ann Owner: Aaron Ballance; Ballance, master; built Hyde Co. 1838; property change; 1 deck, 2 mast, 44 ft. long, 15 ft. wide, 5 ft. deep; 20 Oct. 1839; Schooner.

Mary Owner: John Pike; Pike, master; built New Bern 1837; 1 deck, 2 mast, 69 ft. long, 21 ft. wide, 7 ft. deep, 96 ton; Schooner

Erie Owner: Samuel Dudley; Simpson. master; 56 ft. long; property change.

David W. Farrow Owner: Tilmon Farrow of Ocracoke; Thomas W. Williams, master; built Ocracoke 1842-43, 1deck, 2 mast, 47 ft. long, 15 ft. wide, 5 ft., has a figure head; 8 May 1843.

Paramount Owners: Wallace H. Styron & Simon H. Garrish; Willis W. Styron, master; built Ocracoke 1839; square stern, has a figure head; property change in part; 5 Feb. 1844.

Little John Owners: William Howard & James Best; Best, master; built Hyde Co. 1839; 1 deck, 2 mast 49 ft. long; July 1844.

James Longhoul Owner: William Howard; Howard, master; built New Bern 1841; July 1849; 45 ft long; Schooner.

Paramount Owners: Simon Bragg & Simon H. Garrish; 1846.

Paramount Thomas Bragg & Euphenia Curtis; Bragg, master; 3 Apr. 1847.

Martha H. Styron Owner: Wallace H. Styron; Styron, master; built Carteret Co. 1849; 1 deck, 2 mast, 60 ft. long, 16 ft. wide, 5 ft. deep, 48 ton, figure head; May 1849; surrendered Plymouth, N.C., 29 May 1851—license expired.

Manuneck Owner: John Pike; Josephus Fulcher, master; 49 ft. long; 1849.

Susan Ann Howard Owner: Richard G. Howard; Lockhart Williams, master; built Ocracoke 1847; 51 ft. long, 2 mast, 39 ft. long; April 1851.

Gladiator Owner: Ira C. Gaskins & Robert Gaskins; built Ocracoke 1851; Robert Gaskins, master; 1 deck, 1 mast, 39 ft. long; April 1851.

Parragon Owners: William Howard Sr., Robert P. Wahab, & Job Wahab; Robert P. Wahab, master; owner changed; 62 ft. long, 19 ft. wide, 6 ft. deep, 57 ton, figure head; 1 Apr. 1851.

Two May Owner: Samuel Dudley, of Portsmouth; Alexandra B. Silverton, master; built New Jersey 1843; 64 ft. long; 1853.

Edward G. Hanks Owners: Lockhart Williams & Thomas Bragg; Williams, master; built Plymouth, N.C., 1848; 1deck, 2 mast, 58 ft. long, 17 ft. wide, 4 ft. deep, 42 ton; Schooner; 1853.

Lorena Owners: Augustus Dudley & Christopher T. Styron; Styron, master; built Carteret Co. 1846; enrolled Ocracoke 1853.

Lorena Owners: Christopher T. Styron, Wallace Styron, & James Mayo; July 1853.

Champion Owners: William H. Howard, Tilmon Farrow, & Robert Wahab.

Manumit Owners: George Pike, 3/4 owner & John Pike, 1/4 owner; A.B. Howard, master; 58 ft. long; 1855; Schooner.

Manumit Owners: George Pike, John Pike, & Abner B. Howard; Howard, master; 1856.

Susan Ann Owners: Tilmon Farrow, & Isaac Farrow of Ocracoke; Oct. 1856.

Patron Owners: Daniel Tolson & William Sylvester Tolson, each 1/2 owner; built Carteret Co. 1852; 55 ft. long; Schooner; 1857.

Rival Owner Jacob Gaskill; Gaskill, master; built Currituck 1841; 1 deck, 2 mast, 51 ft. long; Schooner; 6 May 1860.

Record Group #41
Records of the Bureau of Marine Inspection & Navigation National Archives
Certificate of Registry Issued at Ocracoke, N.C.
1816-1844, 1854-1855, 1858-1866

Convent Owners: Jesse Perry of Ocracoke & Richard Winslow, Merchant of Ocracoke; Jesse Perry, 1 master; vessel built at Barnstable, Mass., in 1823; reg. Ocracoke March 1826; 1 deck, 2 mast, 64 ft. long, 18 ft. 7 in. wide, 8ft. 8 in. deep, 69 ton; Schooner.

Henry Waring Owners: Elisha Chase & William Howard of Ocracoke; George Hobbs, master; built at Ocracoke in 1824 with permanent enrollment at this port 29 Oct. 1824, surrendered for this enrollment 1833; 1 deck, 2 mast, 72 ft. long, 22 ft. wide, 7 ft. 4 in. deep, 99 & 87/95 ton; square stem, no gallow, billet head; Schooner.

Surrendered Certificate of Enrollment

Beaufort

1819 *Activ*—G.W. Willis, new vessel; surrendered, Ocracoke 16 Sept. 1822; new owner.

Ocracoke

1819

Jun. 10 *Two Brothers*—William Scarborough; James Bell, master; new vessel; surrendered in Edenton, July 16,1823; new owner.

Sept. 16 *John Wallace*—Richard Gaskill, owner & master; surrendered Jan. 1822; vessel completely lost.

1820

Jul. 6 *Sally Ann*—Richard Winslow, George Jackson, master D. Changed, issued 1819 May 6, Fairfield 50 ton, surrendered Ocracoke July 10, 1822; property transferred.

Jul. 9 *Mariner*—Willis Williams Owner & master; property change, issued May 23, 1819, Edenton; 40 ton; surrendered Ocracoke, Aug. 21, 1821; new owner.

Sept. 8 *Maria*—James Howard Owner & master; new vessel, surrendered, Baltimore; new owner; June 22, 1824.

Oct. 9 *John Burney*—Amasa Styron, George Dixon; changed papers 15 July 1820; 26 ton; surrendered Ocracoke, May 2, 1822; vessel entirely lost

1821

Dec. 15 *Expedition*—Richard Winslow; Samuel Casey, master; change of papers, issued 30 Aug. 1821 Ocracoke; 44 ton; surrendered New Orleans 25 Feb. 1822; vessel totally lost at sea.

1822

Jan. 1 *Eliza*—John S. Howard, owner & master; new vessel; 67 ton; surrendered Ocracoke 15 Jan. 1822.

Jan. 4 *Ann Howard*—John Howard, Tho Hoggart, master; new vessel; 70 ton; surrendered Edenton 2 July 1822.

Jul 26 *JNO*—William Howard; George Williams, master; new owner 16 May 1818; enrolled Portland; surrendered Ocracoke 26 July 1823.

Apr. 17 *Louisa*—James Best Owner & master; papers transferred 20 Mar. 1819; 56 ton; surrendered 24 Aug. 1824, Washington; papers transferred.

Jul. 7 *Sally Ann*—Samuel Casey, owner & master; papers transferred, 6 Jul 1820, Ocracoke; surrendered Edenton; 60 ton; papers transferred.

Oct. 17 *Mariner*—Thomas Bragg, owner; James Gaskill, master; papers transferred 21 Sept. 1821, Ocracoke; 40 ton; surrendered Edenton 15 Sept 1823; papers transferred.

Nov. 30 *George*—William Howard Jr. Owner and Master; new vessel; 24 ton.

New Bern

1823

March *Collector*—Robert Pike Owner & master; enrolled New Bern 24 Jan 1822; 74 ton; surrendered Plymouth 28 Oct. 1823.

Sept. 18 *Sally Ann*—Benjamine Jackson Owner & master.

Ocracoke

1823

Feb. 26 *NPC*—William Howard, owner; Tobios Cook, master; property change in part 7 Feb 1822; enrolled Ocracoke; 48 ton; surrendered Boston 11 Jun. 1823; new owner.

Apr. 1 *Ann Howard*—John Howard, owner & master; change of papers; enrolled Ocracoke, July 1825;

70 ton; surrendered Ocracoke; new owner.

Apr. 28 *Frances*—Richard Winslow, owner; M. Ventass, master, papers changed 21 May 1822, enrolled Plymouth, 60 ton; surrendered, Boston; new owner.

Apr. 30 *Fort Landing*—Benjamine Williams, owner and master; papers changed in part, 8 Sept. 1822; enrolled Boston; 56 tons; surrendered Ocracoke; property change 20 Apr. 1824.

June 30 *Mary*—John Mayo, owner; William Williams, master; vessel stranded Nov. 1822; surrendered Ocracoke 5 May 1823; new owner.

Nov. 28 *Thomas H. Blount*—George Scarborough, owner; James C. Garrish, master; district change; enrolled 18 Mar. 1817, Washington; 29 ton; surrendered Ocracoke 28 Oct. 1826; property change.

1824

July 10 *Hannah*—John Jackson, owner & master; change papers; enrolled 25 June 1824, Norfolk; 44 ton; surrendered Washington 9 April 1827; new owner.

Aug. 24 *Louisa*—N. O'Neal, owner & master; papers transferred 7 Apr. 1822; enrolled Ocracoke; 56 ton; surrendered Washington 1826; new owner.

Aug. 1 *Albert*—Samuel Dudley, owner & master; new vessel; surrendered Elizabeth City 4 Feb. 1833; property changed.

Feb. 23 *Maria*—James Howard, owner & master; 59 ton; new vessel; surrendered Ocracoke 29 Oct. 1824; reissued.

Nov. 11 *Collector*—Robert Pike, master.

April 15 *Convert*—James Howard, owner; new owner; enrolled Barnstable, 69 ton, 31 May 1823; surrendered Wilmington, 31 Oct 1825; reissued.

1824

Jun. 4 *George Washington*—George Scarborough, owner & master; new vessel, enrolled Camden 25 May 1824; reissued.

Oct. 28 *Thomas H. Blount*—William Howard, owner; Samuel Garrish, master; papers transferred, 28 Nov. 1822, Ocracoke; 29 ton; surrendered Ocracoke 1 Dec. 1826; property transferred.

Oct. 29 *Henry Warren*—William Howard, owner; John Roberts, master; new vessel; enrolled Ocracoke; surrendered Ocracoke, 28 Feb. 1833; rebuilt.

Oct. 30 *Brothers & Sisters*—John Howard, owner & master; new vessel; surrendered Ocracoke 1832; changed property.

Nov. 29 *Sadge*—William Scarborough, owner; Joseph Williams, master; new owner enrolled 13 Mar. 1820, Washington; 20 ton; surrendered Washington, 25 Jan. 1826; new owner.

Washington

1825

Apr. 14 *Post Boy*—William Austin, owner & master; new papers, 11 Nov. 1824 issued Washington; surrendered Washington 15 Jun. 1825; new owners.

April 23 *Two Brothers*—Tilmon Farrow, owner & master, new vessel, 55 ton.

Jun. 20 *Convoy*—Hezekiah Farrow, new vessel, 73 ton, surrendered 3 Jan. 1826, Washington, reissued.

Oct. 10 *Two Brothers*—H. Ballance, owner & master, property change, part. enrolled 12 Oct. 1824, Washington, 32 ton, surrendered Washington 18 Nov. 1826. property ch.

Elizabeth City

1825

Mar. 14 *Sally*—Horatio N. Williams, owner; E.B. Hathaway, master; property change; Apr. 1822, Camden; 56 ton; 29 Aug. 1825; vessel altered.

Aug. 29 *Sally*—Altered.

Ocracoke

1825

Jan. 21 *Thomas Cox*—John Pike, master.

Feb. 19 *Planter*—Richard Winslow.

Mar. 31 *Maria*—James Howard, owner; Whitehurst, master; change of papers, 29 Oct. 1824, Ocracoke; 59 ton; surrendered Washington; new owner.

Aug. 15 *George Washington*—William Howard, owner; James Chaplin, master; enrolled 25 May 1825, Camden; 48 ton; surrendered Washington 22 July 1827; reissued.

Sept. 17 *Utility*—Mary Styron, owner; Wallace Styron, master; new vessel, 49 ton; surrendered New Bern 12 July 1829; new owner.

1826

Mar. 14 *Collector*—Isaac Farrow, owner & master, 25 Nov. 1825, Camden; 75 ton; surrendered Camden; reissued.

Apr. 12 *Leopard*—Thomas A. Smith, owner; Caleb Ballence, master; new owner, 4 Nov. 1825, Beaufort; 24 ft.; surrendered Washington 19 July 1826; reissued.

Mar. 24 *Convert*—Richard Winslow, owner; Joe Wahab, master; enrolled 18 Jan. 1826, Ocracoke, 61 ton; surrendered Ocracoke 11 Nov. 1827; reissued.

May 15 *Maria*—James Howard, owner & master; enrolled Ocracoke 17 Feb. 1826; 59 ft.; surrendered Ocracoke 3 July 1826; reissued.

July 17 *Sidney*—George Howard, owner & master; new owner; enrolled 26 Dec. 1825, Washington; 20 ton; surrendered Ocracoke, 22 Dec. 1838; property change in part.

Nov. 23 *William*—Jacob Gaskill, owner & master; new owner; enrolled 26 December 1825, Washington; 20 ton; surrewndered Ocracoke, 22 Dec. 1838; property change in part.

1827

Mar. 28 *Olivia Cox*—Thomas Cox, owner; Robert Pike, master; new vessel; 99 ton; surrendered N.Y. 14 July 1827.

Dec. 4 *Olivia Cox*—Robert Pike, owner & master; new owner enrolled N.Y. 14 July 1827; 99 ton; surrendered 4 Apr. 1828 Edenton; new owner.

Feb. 13 *Industry*—William Howard, owner & master; new vessel; enrolled Camden 20 Oct. 1822.

Apr. 2 *Henry*—Bateman O'Neal, owner; James C. Garrish, master; enrolled Edenton 15 Sept. 1820; 40 ton; surrendered Washington June 1829; owner transferred in part.

May 21 *Active*—E. Styron, owner, S Dixon, master; new owner May 21, 1827, Ocracoke; 32 ton.

1828

Jan. 3 *Henry Bateman*—O'Neal, owner; James C. Garrish, master; vessel altered, 20 Apr. 1826; property part transferred, Ocracoke, 2 July 1830.

Jul. 27 *Two Brothers*—Holloway Ballance, owner & master; property part transferred 27 Nov. 1826, Washington; 32 ton; part transferred 29 Mar. 1829.

Sept. 12 *James G. Stacy*—George Howard, owner; George Hobbs, master; new owner, 15 May 1827, Georgetown, 74 ton, part transferred 2 Oct. 1829, Ocracoke.

Sept. 25 *Olixia Bricketh*—William Howard, owner; Benjamine Williams, mater; new vessel.

Nov. 5 *Fr. L. Kennedy*—John Howard, owner; Thomas Smith, master; new vessel; 99 ton; surrendered Washington 14 Aug. 1830; reissued.

1829

Apr. 14 *William A. Blount*—Tilmon Farrow, owner & master; new vessel; 35 ton; surrendered Charleston 1832; reissued.

Jan. 3 *Thomas H. Blount*—Simon H. Garrish, owner; Joseph Williams, master; part transferred, Jan. 1828, Ocracoke; surrendered Camden 2 July 1831; new owner.

July 4 *Wesleyan*—Thomas Bragg, owner & master; part transferred 1826 Ocracoke; 29 ton; surrendered Camden 1832, new owner.

Oct. 3 *Lorant*—William Howard, owner; Elisha Chase, master; new vessel; 30 ton; Ocracoke.

1830

Mar. 30 *Epex*—Jacob Gaskill, owner & master; new owner, 16 Feb. 1828, Beaufort; 45 on; surrendered Ocracoke 23 Aug. 1832; reissued.

1833

June 7 *Leopard*—Holloway Ballance, owner & master; new owner.

Nov. 12 *Lorant*—William Howard, owner; Francis Jackson, master.

1834

Aug. 4 *Louis Ann*—Christopher O'Neal, owner; Holloway Ballance, master; part change 25 May 1832, New Bern; 28 ton; surrendered Ocracoke 25 Oct. 1839; papers transferred.

1836

May 31 *Hope*—Ira C. Gaskins; new owner; surrendered 1839.

Jun. 15 *Brothers & Sisters*—Blackwell; new owner.

Nov. 13 *Convoy*—Simpson; new owner.

Nov. 18 *Henry Bateman*—George Hobbs, owner & master; new owner- Sloop.

1838

Feb. 15 *Union*—R. Jones, owner; Thomas Bragg, master; new vessel; 36 ton.

1840

Jan. 8 *Nancy*—Christopher O'Neal, owner & master; new vessel; 36 ton.

Feb. 12 *Mary*—John Pike, owner & master; property change; surrendered 2 Mar. 1840; vessel lost.

Sept. 2 *Union*—John Pike, property change.

CHAPTER 10

Seafaring Men

SEAMEN OR SEAFARING MEN OF OCRACOKE (EXCLUDING PILOTS & FISHERMEN)

Seamen Listed In 1850 census

Name	Age	Name	Age
Elisha Ballance	age 26	Willis W. Styron	27
John Gaskins	23	Job Wahab	48
Francis O'Neal	42	Thomas Wahab	21
Thomas Styron	56	William Wahab	20
Wallace Styron	56	Lockhart Williams	36

In addition there were in 1850

26 pilots　　1 lighthouse keeper　　1 clerk

25 laborers	4 merchants
4 fishermen	5 mechanics

Seafaring Men of 1860

Oliver Bragg	62	Franklin Howard	40
George Howard	20	W.B. Harvy	48
Samuel Bailey	25	Wm. Wahab	30
Amon Howard	40	Thomas Styron	37
A.B. Howard	29	Jacob Garrish	15
William Bragg	21	James Garrish	45
Burruss Bragg	21	Thomas Jackson	23

Capt. Thurston Gaskill on the *South Wind*, Ocracoke Lighthouse in center background. Boat has oil-burning lights on top of cabin (ca. 1940).

DAVID GASKILL COLLECTION

Men oystering in North Pond.

ELLEN ROBINSON COLLECTION

J.B. Austin	45	Zora B Gaskins	30
Alonzo Howard	19	Jamie Styron	41
James Howard	21	Robert Gaskins	44
John Williams	46	Holloway Ballance	15
Jacob Gaskill	76	Elijah Gaskins	26
James Spencer	30	George Gaskins	21
Willis Bragg	22	Washington Gaskins	40
Harris Howard	24	Wallace Simpson	48
Wm. S. Tolson	34	J.W. Williams	18
Benj. O'Neal	53	Nathaniel Bragg	16
Howard Jackson	48	Lockhart Wms.	49
Benj. Gaskins	40	Thomas Tolson	45
W.H. Gaskins	36	William O'Neal	32
Wm. Fulcher	18	W.S. Gaskill	50
Benj. Garrish	17		

In addition there were in 1860

4 carpenters
16 pilots
1 master carpenter
1 fisherman

Upper row: Men hanging and drying nets, 1950s.
Lower row: Fishermen cleaning seaweed from nets.
ALL PHOTOS, ELLEN ROBINSON COLLECTION.
UPPER RIGHT PHOTO AND LOWER PHOTO, DIGITAL IMAGES COURTESY CORE SOUND WATERFOWL MUSEUM AND HERITAGE CENTER

Seafaring Men of 1870

Munroe Bragg	21	James Jackson	25
Samuel D. Bragg	34	Thomas Jackson	45
Sanderson Bragg	23	Joseph O'Neal	36
Benjamine Garrish	26	Simon O'Neal	33
Jacob Garrish	24	Thad Scarborough	32
James Garrish	21	Benjamine Spencer	41
George Gaskins	25	William Toler	40
James Howard	32	William Wahab	40
Wallis Howard	30	Uriah Wahab	24
Henderson Jackson	25	Horatio Williams	43
Gilbert O'Neal	22		

In addition there were in 1870:

5 pilots
1 mechanic
1 miller
11 laborers
14 fishermen
1 carpenter
3 merchants
1 teacher
1 member of legislature

Sailors of 1880

Aaron Ballance	30	John W. O'Neal	24
Herbert H. Ballance	40	Franklin W. O'Neal	20
William Ballance	61	Wm. M. O'Neal	32
Richard C. Lawrence	50	Christopher O'Neal	31
Basil B. Bragg	41	Epheriam O'Neal	26
James M. Bragg	50	Christopher O'Neal	31
Samuel D. Bragg	44	Warren W. O'Neal	26
Thomas Bragg	42	Robert L. O'Neal	20
Winslow S. Bragg	32	B.B. O'Neal	18
Edward F. Fulcher	17	Christopher Scarborough	26
George L. Fulcher	35	Wm. D. Scarborough	23
John G. Fulcher	29	Thad Scarborough	41
Benjamine Garrish	36	George W. Simpson	28
Benjamine Gaskill	41	A. Williams	25

Shrimping in Pamlico Sound, 1948.

NORTH CAROLINA MARITIME MUSEUM

Shrimp boats off Ocracoke

POST CARD, CIRCA 1960

Thomas R. Gaskill	25	Sommers Spencer	33
Benjamine Gaskill	26	John W. Spencer	21
William W. Gaskins	30	Amos Howard	60
Thomas Gaskins	27	Thomas D. Howard	28
Zorable Gaskins	25	Amon Howard	26
Amasa G. O'Neal	48	Abner Howard	19
Benjamine Fulcher	34	William E. Howard	22
Tillmon O'Neal	33	James W. Howard	41
Perry C. Howard	44	James N. Williams	25
Simon B. Howard	50	Wm. J. Gaskins	29
John W. Howard	17	Richard C. Williams	37
William A. Jackson	22	David Williams	22
Henderson Jackson	36	David M. Williams	58
Benjamine Williams	30	Warren Williams	23
David Williams	26	Millard F. Williams	29
Horatio Williams	42		

In addition there were in 1880

28 fishermen	1 pilot
1 carpenter	12 teachers
3 clammers	1 mail carrier

Census of 1900

By now, the U.S. Lifesaving Service had been established on Ocracoke. The days of shipping through Ocracoke Inlet were over. Men began to find work that would let them stay home. There were only eighteen sailors. There were twenty-four fishermen, eleven oystermen, and eight with the U.S. Life-Saving Service.

Sailors

Fred W. Bragg	Richard F. O'Neal
Norman Garrish	Hubbart O'Neal
Jacob Garrish	Alpheus Simpson
George W. Gaskill	Horatio Williams
James L. Gaskill	Thomas Williams

View of the harbor from behind the second old post office, circa 1950s.

OCRACOKE PRESERVATION SOCIETY,
MARY RUTH JONES DICKSON COLLECTION

Tide is out and boats are high and dry in this 1957 photograph. Some of creek that would become Silver Lake has not yet been dredged. Ponies are still roaming free.

PHOTO BY BERTHA GARRISH O'NEAL, OCRACOKE PRESERVATION SOCIETY

Wm. D. Gaskill
Martin Harris
Lloyd Simpson
Jordan Williams
Benj. D. Gaskill

Fishermen

Alexander Garrish
James S. Garrish
Henry Garrish
Preston Garrish
Simon Garrish
John Gaskill
Thomas F. Gaskins
William J. Gaskins
George W. Jackson
Howard F. O'Neal
William W. O'Neal
Luther O'Neal
George W. Simpson Jr.
Stacy Simpson
Nathan Spencer

Oystermen

Gary Bragg
Christopher Garrish
Benjamine B. O'Neal
Christopher O'Neal
William B. O'Neal
Tilmon W. O'Neal
Isham H. Simpson
Willialm D. Simpson
Andrew S. Simpson
John W. Spencer
David T. Tolson
Daniel B. Garrish
Benjamine O'Neal
Elihu Spencer
Andrew Spencer, Jr.
Edward Spencer
William T. Spencer, age 74

Waterman

Perry C. Howard

USLSS

Robert W. Gaskill
James H. Howard
Charlie McWilliams
George Simpson
James H. Wahab
David Williams
George L. Fulcher
George L. Fulcher Jr.

Fishermen

Elijan Styron
Thomas Tolson
Warren W. Williams

Lighthouse Keeper
Tilmon F. Smith

Navy
James H. Garrish

Boat Builder
Thomas M. O'Neal

Net Maker
John B. Gaskins

Also in 1900 there were

2 ministers
6 carpenters
1 teacher
2 merchants
2 laborers
1 RR agent
2 pilots
1 manufacturer
4 dressmakers

CHAPTER 11

U.S. Life-Saving Service

The United States Life-Saving Service was first established around the Great Lakes in 1847. It was not until 1874 that it expanded to North Carolina's Outer Banks with the construction of seven stations. Within ten years the number of stations grew to twenty-nine.

Harper's Monthly Magazine, in an issue published February 1882, featured a story on *The American Life-Saving Service*. The story began:

> No subject at the present moment is more replete with vital and romantic interest at home and abroad than that of the American Life-Saving Service. Its brief his-

tory teams with incident and instruction. Its wonderful achievements have given it wide celebrity the world over and foreign journals are advocating the adoption of its methods in European countries.

There have been three stations on Ocracoke Island. The first was commissioned in 1883 and located on the north tip of the island. It was known as the Hatteras Inlet Station. Many daring rescues were made by the crew of this station. The seventy-year-old station had to be evacuated and decommissioned in 1953 because the station was about to fall into the ocean due to severe erosion. The ocean finally claimed it in the summer of 1955.

There have been two stations in the village of Ocracoke located near "the Ditch." The first station, commissioned in 1914, was located on and faced Pamlico Sound. A new

Ocracoke Coast Guard Station, built in the 1940s.

AUTHOR COLLECTION, DIGITAL PRINT COURTESY OF CORE SOUND WATERFOWL MUSEUM AND HERITAGE CENTER station was built during World War II and the old one was torn down.

All three of these stations were manned with a crew of local men. The chief in charge was appointed, and he was responsible for getting his crew from the local community. These men risked their lives in daring attempts to save the lives of seamen and civilians alike.

These men had to stand watch in the tower of the station around the clock. They had to patrol the beach at night, regardless of the weather, to watch for ships in distress.

It must be remembered that this was a time before the modern well-equipped Coast Guard cutters of today. There were only lifeboats with oars and manpower. The lifeboats were pulled to the ocean side with horses or mules. They were launched by men wading through the surf and jumping aboard after the boat made it through the breakers. If a ship was wrecked on the beach, a line was shot to the vessel with a Lyle Gun. After the line was secured on the vessel, a life-car (see illustration) was attached. The life-car was then sent out to the ship. The crew and passengers, two or three at a time, climbed into the car, closed the hatch, and were pulled to shore by surfmen on the beach. In severe weather this operation could take several days.

Life-Saving crew members have had their hands and feet frozen, had severe rope bums, collapsed with fatigue, and gone without food for days. They may have spent hours swimming in a stormy ocean to bring back a stranded sailor.

These "Heroes of the Surf" were a breed of their own: they were *Old Salts*. They had salt water in their veins.

On January 28, 1915, the Life-Saving Service was joined with the Revenue Service and became the United States Coast Guard. The Coast Guard continues the traditions begun by the Life-Saving Service. Visitors to Ocracoke have often witnessed first-hand the services rendered by

Ocracoke's three Life-Saving/Coast Guard stations

From top:

- **Hatteras Inlet Station, 1883-1955,** north end of island, Ocracoke side of inlet;
- **Ocracoke Station, 1914-1940s,** south end of island, located near Ditch
- **Ocracoke Coast Guard Station, 1940s,** south end of island, still in operation.[1]

PHOTOS FROM ELIZABETH HOWARD COLLECTION

1 PUBLISHER'S NOTE: The Coast Guard station would be vacated in 1996, the year after the publication of *Old Salt*. It now houses the North Carolina Center for the Advancement of Teaching.

this valiant group. Almost every resident of Ocracoke has either retired from the service or is related to someone who has been connected to the Coast Guard. The station in the village is a constant reminder of our seafaring heritage.

Some Ocracoke men who served with the U.S. Life-Saving Service:

George L. Fulcher	R.F. Howard
George L. Fulcher, Jr.	Wheeler Howard
Benjamine J. Garrish	Andrew Jackson
James H. Garrish	Charlie S. McWilliams
Simon Garrish	B.G. O'Neal
G.M. Gaskill	Charlie M. O'Neal
Robert W. Gaskill	F. O'Neal
G.B. Gaskins	Isaac O'Neal
Matthew Guthrie	Jesse W. O'Neal
Hatten H. Howard	Richard F. O'Neal
James W. Howard	Stanly O'Neal

The Lyle Gun came into use by the Life-Saving Service for rescues from shipwrecks. On the Atlantic coast in hurricane season and during winter storms, the ocean is much too fierce to attempt a rescue by boat. The idea of throwing a line from the shore to a ship in distress was first suggested by Lieutenant Bell of the Royal Artillery in 1791.

The first gun used 288 pounds of cast iron that could throw a ball with an attached line 421 yards. The gun had to be pulled by horse and cart to the ocean side, through deep sand. This was very difficult, especially on the Outer Banks of North Carolina, where there is mile after mile of deep dry sand.

Lieutenant D.A. Lyle was appointed by the service to solve the problem of weight and distance of line throwing. In 1878 he came up with "the Lyle Gun," made of bronze, weighing 185 pounds, and having a range of 695 yards. The gun had a shank with an eye protruding from the muzzle where the shot line was tied.

The shot line was coiled in a box in such order that it could be shot to a wreck without being tangled. It was made of unbleached linen thread, braided and waterproofed. It was shot in a direction to fall across the ship, after which one end was secured on the ship and another end on the beach. A double pulley-block was used to draw a breeches-buoy to and fro on the ropes, bringing one person at a time to safety on the beach.

This seems to be a fairly simple task to perform, but it must be remembered that these ships were usually wrecked during storms, with gales of wind, rain, or ice, or at night, when visibility was not good. Shooting out a line against gale force winds to a wrecked or beached ship that rises, rolls, and half turns over with every gust is no easy task.

Members of the life-saving crew were often dragged into the surf, hands bleeding from rope bums. In winter every spray of water froze until they were covered with ice. They risked their lives every day to save others.

The Life-Saving Car also was used by the Life-Saving Service for rescues. The life-saving car, better known as the Life-Car, was a small covered boat made of sheet-iron, into which six or seven people could be brought from a distressed vessel to safety on the beach.

The Lyle Gun was used to shoot out lines to the ship on which the Life-Car could be drawn back and forth. The Life Car was harder to handle, because it weighed much more than the breeches-buoy, but it was more effective when large numbers of people had to be rescued and extreme haste was required.

This does not mean it was the safest way to be rescued. Many survivors of shipwrecks were treated for bruises and

Tools of every surfman's trade in the U.S. Life-Saving Service, forerunner to the Coast Guard: the life boat, the Lyle Gun and the Life-Saving Car. The original Life Car used by the Ocracoke station can be seen on the lawn of the Ocracoke Museum Visitors Center.

DRAWINGS BY ELLEN FULCHER CLOUD

broken bones after a rolling and tumbling trip in the spinning Life-Car.

Some would rather perish on board the ship than get into the car. Such was the case of a woman who was the cook on the *Hartzel* in Lake Michigan in October of 1880. Refusing to get into the Life-Car each time it was sent out, and watching the car spin in the air and finally come to rest upside down in the surf, she lashed herself to the mast saying she "didn't want to get into that thing, it looks too much like a coffin." The mast soon fell and her body was found seventeen days later at Frankfort.

JOSEPH W. ETHERIDGE,

Superintendent of 6th Life-Saving Service District, Chesapeake Bay to Cape Fear River, July 2, 1878–June 16, 1885 and Jan. 10, 1890–Feb. 15, 1893

•

From the *Annual Report of the Operations of the United States Life-saving Service for the Fiscal Year Ending June 30, 1893*:

DEATH OF SUPERINTENDENT ETHERIDGE

By the death of Captain Joseph W. Etheridge, superintendent of the Sixth Life-Saving District at Beaufort, North Carolina, February 15, 1893, the Service suffered the loss of a competent and zealous officer. Captain Etheridge was born in Chowan County, near Edenton, North Carolina, in the vicinity of Albemarle Sound, August 14, 1839. Located by the accident of birth in the vicinity of expansive interior waters communicationing with the ocean, he made himself thoroughly acquainted in his youth with the bays, sounds and coasts of his native State and acquired a nautical experience that served him in good stead in the business of later life.

In early manhood Captain Etheridge taught school in the vicinity of Edenton. During the civil war he served awhile as an officer in the Union Army and later as a pilot upon United States gunboats. He also served a term in the legislature of North Carolina. He followed the business of a fisherman and merchant for many years, and came in contact with a large number of people, whose respect and good will he enjoyed for his substantial character and kindly disposition.

He was for ten years superintendent of the Sixth Life-Saving District, embracing all of the stations on the North Carolina coast, as well as those on the shore of Virginia south of Cape Henry, and proved himself vigorous and efficient.

While on a tour of duty, making a winter's journey among the bleak and isolated coast of North Carolina, he contracted pneumonia, which ran to a speedy and fatal termination.

CHAPTER 12

When the Sound Froze Over[1]

Joseph W. Etheridge was a resident of the Roanoke Island when he posted bond of $35,000 to secure his position as Superintendent of Life Saving of our area. The 1880 census list him as being 42 years of age and his occupation was listed as Supt. LSS. Living in his household were his wife, Martha J., age 45; two daughters, age 8 and 13; his father Daniel, age 70, minister; and brother Daniel, age 28, seaman USLSS.

The territory of which he was superintendent extended from Chesapeake Bay to Cape Fear River, which included 29 stations, with distances between them of 285 miles. These stations, which are situated upon an extremely wild

1 PUBLISHER'S NOTE: This chapter was a separate article the author wrote after the publication of ***Old Salt***.

Boats on a partially frozen Silver Lake, February 1958. Not even that cold spell came close to comparing with the deadly freeze of 1893.

NATIONAL PARK SERVICE, CAPE HATTERAS NATIONAL SEASHORE

and desolate coast, involved great preservation and hardship to traverse, especially in winter. His duty required him to visit at least every three months to inspect their condition and to pay their crews.

During one of these trips, he contracted a disease from which he died. It was in January of 1893 that Superintendent Etheridge became stranded at Ocracoke, unable to proceed on his trip to inspect the stations and pay the crew because of a severe winter storm and the freezing of Pamlico and Core sounds.

By this time Etheridge had been widowed, married a second wife and had three small children who remained at home and were waiting for his return.

His stay at Ocracoke was cold and lonesome, but his visit to Portsmouth Island was only to get worse.

It was a bitter cold day in January when Joseph Gaskill[2] anchored his schooner at Ocracoke, intending to wait out this winter freeze.

Upon hearing of his arrival, Etheridge, being anxious to proceed, approached Gaskill, offering to pay him well if he would take him to New Bern, N.C. in his schooner. Gaskill agreed and, after taking Etheridge aboard, they took sail to cross Pamlico Sound. They got only a short distance through the ice, were blocked, and then drifted back to Ocracoke with the tide. Supintendent Etheridge, still being determined to proceed, instructed Joseph Gaskill to purchase a pony-and-road cart, which they took in the schooner across Ocracoke Inlet, the ice in the inlet being broken by the current.

They landed at Portsmouth, N.C., on the afternoon of January 23, and made a start on the beach for Cape Lookout Station. They made 10 miles of the journey that afternoon. Before night they stopped at the only dwelling on the route of 46 miles and took dinner. They then prepared to make another start but the horse got away from them, pulling the cart as he went. After much to-do, they finally se-

2 Note, there were two Joseph Gaskills in the area at this time, one a resident of Portsmouth, the other a resident of Hog Island. Have not yet determined which one this is.

cured the horse, but the cart was broken and beat to pieces. The horse was so much disabled that they were compelled to remain at the dwelling overnight.

The next morning they had hoped to procure a boat to take them over to the mainland but that was impossible. The sound was frozen. Failing in this, they borrowed an ox cart from the dwelling and hitched it to the horse and proceeded, one walking while the other rode, the weather being so severe it was necessary to exercise to keep from freezing.

Night overtook them about 10 miles from Cape Lookout and they had no choice but to stop at a deserted fish camp on the beach. Finding no wood, they had to tear the sides from the camp for firewood. The camp had no floor, so they built a fire on the ground of the camp and cut rushes to cover the ground on which they sat. They had only one blanket, with which Joseph Gaskill covered Etheridge while Gaskill kept up the fire as best he could.

Etheridge, being very tired and worn out from exposure, dropped off to sleep about 8 o'clock, only to awake at 9:40, asking what time it was. He complained that he was sick and they must move, declaring that he could not live until daylight if they stayed where they were. He then had a chill, followed by a severe headache and fever. However, they were compelled to stay, having no other place of refuge they could reach.

As soon as day broke, they started for Cape Lookout Station and arrived there about 10 a.m. after walking 10 miles. The horse was worn out and unable to pull either of them. At the station, they were supplied with food and taken in a cart to a small settlement on the banks near Beaufort. There they were put in a boat and arrived at Beaufort the 25th day of January at 5 p.m.

Superintendent Etheridge continued sick through the whole trip and died just a few days after reaching Beaufort. Joseph Gaskill reported that his experience on this trip was more severe than any which he had encountered during twenty years as a seaman.

ALETA

CHAPTER 13

Another Old Salt and His Vessel

There is another *Old Salt* who needs to be recognized here, my father, Captain Elmo Fulcher. He was born on November 13, 1912, in Harkers Island, North Carolina. He was a commercial fisherman, and while fishing at Ocracoke, he met and married Lillian Jackson, my mother. They had three children, Elmo Murray, Jr., Ellen Marie, and Laurie Moore. They made Ocracoke their home.

Like many other islanders, he spent his entire life working on the water. In the 1940s he became mate and relief captain for Captain Wilbur Nelson on the famed mail boat *Aleta*, which ran the mail from Ocracoke to Atlan-

Mailboat *Aleta*, waiting to take on mail at Portsmouth. The author, her father and her brother are on bow.

AUTHOR COLLECTION

Aleta leaving Atlantic, N.C. (late 1940s). Notice how low in the water the boat sits. The passengers filled the rear cabin and the stem. The front cabin was filled with mail and freight On the upper deck, passengers were shoulder to shoulder under the canopy and others had to sit on fish boxes on top of the front cabin.

AUTHOR COLLECTION

Aleta at dock in Atlantic, waiting to take on mail and passengers.

OUTER BANKS HISTORY CENTER, MANTEO., N.C., AYCOCK BROWN COLLECTION

Mailboat *Aleta*.

ELIZABETH HOWARD COLLECTION

tic, North Carolina, daily. This was before paved roads and ferry service to the island. The *Aleta* was the main source of communication with the outside world for the island. It was built in 1923 by Ambrose Fulcher for Howard Nelson to run the mail from Morehead City to Atlantic. Captain Nelson named the boat for his sister. When the highway was built from Beaufort to Atlantic, the *Aleta* was sold and became a booze runner. She was seized by federal agents and auctioned off. Dee Mason of Atlantic bought her for a buy boat[1]. In 1938, Captain Wilbur Nelson bought her to run the mail to Ocracoke.

During World War II, Captain Nelson, Captain Elmo Fulcher, and the *Aleta* served their country by carrying the necessary freight, mail, and passengers for the Navy, Army, Coast Guard, as well as civilians, to and from the island. While ships could be seen burning off the coast, the *Aleta* slowly crossed the inlet from Portsmouth to Ocracoke. Often her captain watched enemy subs surface just yards away.

In 1945 Captain Elmo and Captain George O'Neal (also of Ocracoke) bought the *Aleta* from Captain Nelson and continued the thirty-mile route, dropping off mail at Portsmouth and Cedar Island. In 1950, the highway was extended from Atlantic to Cedar Island, making this stop no longer necessary.

In 1952, Captain Elmo and Captain George lost the mail contract and Captain Elmo bought Captain George's half of the boat. He converted it to a shrimp trawler and continued to use it until his death in 1979.

The mail route is history now with the many ferries that run daily to Ocracoke, but the *Aleta* has left her mark in history. It is not unusual to see a painting or sketch of her as a trawler in an art exhibit. There are hand-carved models

---

1 ***buy boat***: a boat that purchases fish, etc., from other boats and takes them to market.

All Captain Elmo's children are *Old Salts*. Pictured here is his son Laurie Fulcher standing on a ferry watching the shrimp trawler owned by his brother, Murray Fulcher. Murray now owns and operates South Point Seafood (fish house) at Ocracoke. Laurie now operates a shrimp trawler that he and I own, the *Capt. Elmo*.

PHOTOS, AUTHOR COLLECTION

Laurie Fulcher rigging the *Capt. Elmo* for shrimping; U.S. Coast Guard station in background.

Mail boat *Aleta* (left), after being converted to a shrimp trawler, docked beside Murray Fulcher's trawler, the *She-Don-Di*, in Silver Lake at Ocracoke, 1970s.

PHOTOS, AUTHOR COLLECTION

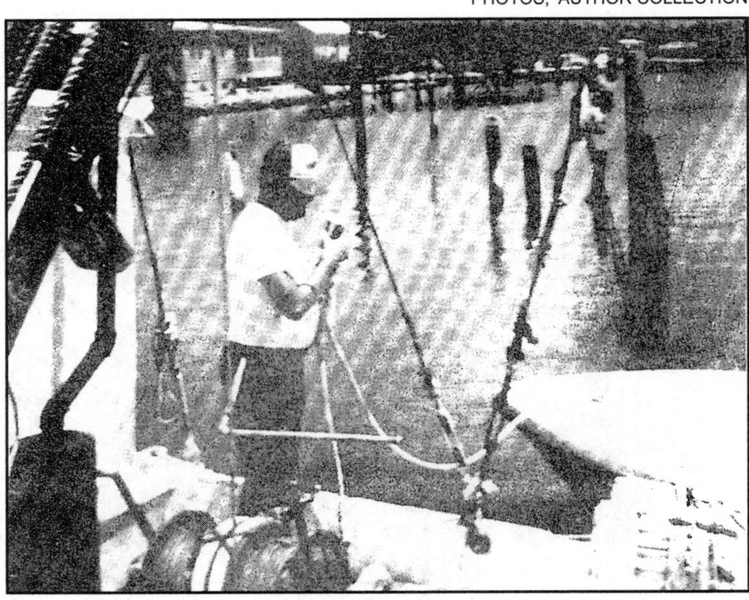

Captain Elmo's son Murray Fulcher, on deck of the *Aleta*, which was converted to a shrimp trawler.

of her displayed around the island. There are also the many men, young and old, who worked as a mate on her with my father.

Captain Elmo was known for his knowledge of the local waters. He needed only the stars or a pocket watch and compass to navigate the sounds of eastern North Carolina.

George Jackson[2] tells about a day that he ran on the mail boat with my father, when the fog was so thick they could not see the bow of the boat. He will be quick to remind you that the trip from here to Cedar Island is a pretty straight stretch, but when you enter Core Sound and head for Atlantic, North Carolina, there is a lot of turning and winding. He tells how Captain Elmo used his pocket watch to time his distance from one marker to another. He used his compass to set his course for the next marker and blew the horn to warn other boaters of their location.

George goes on to tell how he heard the captain back down on the engine, while giving the boat a turn to the left, and then he let the engine idle. He asked Captain Elmo what was going on and why had he stopped the boat. The reply was, "Well, George, we're here. We're at the dock in Atlantic." George stuck his head out of the window and could see nothing, but he could hear a car running and people talking on the dock.

Many years later, while visiting my parents, we were listening to the CB radio and heard a trawler in trouble. The weather was very stormy and visibility was about zero because of blowing rain and heavy surf. The trawler's pilot was trying to get in through Ocracoke Inlet. His radar was out and he feared the shoals and sand bars in the inlet. The

---

2 George Guthrie Jackson is brother to the author's mother, Lillian Jackson Fulcher.

SHRIMP BOATS AND
THEIR OWNERS
OPERATING
OUT OF OCRACOKE
IN THE LATE 1950S:

Gregg .... Maltby Bragg
Yvette .... Gary Bragg
Selma W. .... Ben Spencer
Stella .... Summers Spencer
Aleta .... Elmo Fulcher
Armeda .... Irvin Forbs
Dryden .... Jesse Garrish
Norma .... Travis Williams
A.B. .... Penta Williams
Ilene .... Stanley Wahab
Silver Lake .... Albert Styron
South Wind ... Thurston Gaskill
Miss Hatteras .. Oscar Burrus
Cecila Ann ..... Travis Williams
Ellen Marie .... Elmo Fulcher
Louise M . ..... Henry Bragg
John Tilden ..... Eph Esham
King Fisher .... Uriah Garrish
Summers .... Stanley Wahab

TODAY (1995), THERE ARE
ONLY TWO:

Miss Meriam .. Nathan Spencer
Capt. Elmo ...... Laurie Fulcher
and Ellen Fulcher Cloud

Shrimp Boat
at Ocracoke
1950

In the early 1950s there were nineteen shrimp boats owned and operated by local fishermen. This number began to decrease in 1957 and after "the big freeze in 1958." When the ferry service began between Ocracoke and Atlantic, North Carolina, in 1959, the fish companies in Atlantic stopped sending buy boats to the island. About the same time, our local ice plant ceased to operate; this made it hard to keep seafood until a truck could get here on the ferry, which at that time made one round trip daily, four hours each way. By 1960, Capt. Elmo Fulcher was the only shrimper on the island.

weather was so bad that the Coast Guard could not get out to him.

My father got up from his chair, put on his coat and hat, and left the house. In a short time, we heard him on the radio, calling the trawler in trouble. He got the boat's location and began to give instructions on what course to steer and for how long, then the next course and so on, until he brought it to dock in the creek. I think that was one of the proudest moments in my life.

Never a day went by but my father left the supper table and went directly to the *Aleta*, to wash her down, paint, mend net, or tinker with the engine. My mother would smile as he went out and say, "He's got to go tell her goodnight."

He was a man of dry humor with a sparkle in his eye. Every man who has ever worked with him seems to have a fond memory of some fishing experience they shared together, and you can bet they will be glad to tell at least one funny tale on him.

He was a plain, hard-working, down-to-earth man, my father—an *Old Salt*.

Elmo Fulcher at the Pigott Railways in Gloucester, early 1970s. Captain Elmo Fulcher plotted his course with the stars, a compass, and his pocket watch.

AUTHOR COLLECTION

The *Capt. Elmo*,
owned by Laurie Fulcher and Ellen Fulcher Cloud.
AUTHOR COLLECTION

Acknowledgments

First, I want to thank my parents for bringing me into this world on the island of Ocracoke, for bringing me up in a home filled with *Old Salts*, for my love for the sea, this island, and everything around it, and for my rich heritage and deep roots on this island. I thank Paulette Chitwood, Agnes Wren, and Ginny Micket of Live Oak Publications for all their help and support in publishing this book and all the *Old Salts* who inspired it.

E.F.C.

PART III

MATERIALS

PHOTOGRAPH BY AYCOCK BROWN, 1954,
OCRACOKE PRESERVATION SOCIETY, COCHRAN COLLECTION

APPENDIX A

RECORDS OF THE COMMISSIONER OF THE REVENUE IN THE DEPARTMENT OF THE TREASURY RELATING TO THE CONSTRUCTION OF OCRACOKE LIGHTHOUSE.

SECOND CONGRESS. SESS. II. CH. 27, 1793.

CHAP. XXVII.—*An Act supplementary to the act for the establishment and support of lighthouses, beacons, buoys, and public piers.*

SECTION 1. *Be it enacted by the Senate and House of Representatives of the United States of America in Congress assembled,* That all expenses, which shall accrue from the first day of July next inclusively, for the necessary support, maintenance and repairs of all lighthouses, beacons, buoys, the stakeage of channels on the sea-coast, and public piers, shall continue to be defrayed by the United States, until the first day of July, in the year one thousand seven hundred and ninety-four, notwithstanding such lighthouses, beacons, or public piers, with the lands and tenements thereunto belonging, and the jurisdiction of the same shall not, in the mean time, be ceded to, or vested in the United States, by the state or states respectively, in which the same may be; and that the said time be further allowed to the states respectively, to make such cession.

SEC. 2. *And be it further enacted,* That the Secretary of the Treasury be authorized and directed to cause a floating beacon or buoy to be provided and placed on Smith's Point shoal, in the Chesapeak bay, and a beacon or floating buoy at the southwest straddle on the Royal shoal, near Ocracoke inlet, in North Carolina.

APPROVED, March 2, 1793.

An act supplementary to the act for the establishment and support of lighthouses, beacons, buoys, and public piers, March 2, 1793.

TREASURY

SIR:

I have the honor to communicate to you, the result of
house on Occracock island, or elsewhere near the entrance of
pense," pursuant to the order of the Senate of the 28th of Marc

The necessary examinations were directed to be made, in
mation on which a report could have been transmitted to the
their order was made. But the difficulty of procuring a co
delay, until June last; and the sickness and death of the collec
an inspector, increased the impediments.

Two ideas prevail upon the subject of a new light on that
house or beacon, should be erected upon the land ceded by the
which, it is supposed, could be effected for the sum of one tho
condly, that a stone light-house, of the first rate, should rather
which, considering former precedents, and the enhanced rates
thousand dollars.

The inducements which occur in favor of erecting the s
position which was indicated by the Legislature of the State, a
to vessels which make Occracock inlet late in the afternoon,
expense of the two buildings, towards which the inquiry neces

The inducements to the erection of the larger light-house,
gation on that coast, by reason of the numerous shoals, and t
2d. The accommodation it will afford to the vessels which ar
marle sounds, including that of Occracock. 3d. The accomm
which ply between the States lying north and those lying sout
trading with the European settlements in the West India isla
of our territory, and to those employed in the transatlantic tra

The traders of North Carolina, so far as could be ascertain
on Cape Hatteras. It is therefore probable, that it would appe
be made; and it may be observed, that, in appropriating the n
to consider, in connection with local circumstances, those wh
national commerce. To these considerations the Legislature
led in making an appropriation of their own funds.

Particular attention was directed to the nature of the grou
case the Legislature should determine to authorize the buildi
foundations, without the least appearance of quicksands.

In regard to *the general expediency* of erecting a light-hous
of the Senate, the affirmative opinion is supported by the reaso
ceding comparison. To those it may be added, that a profit
war, will be promoted by the establishment of light-houses on
United States will be led thereby to navigate through and acr
[illegible], or hostile cruisers of greater draughts of water
shoals and banks on the eastern coasts, frequently protected u
greater size and strength, during the late war.

I have the honor to be, with great respect, sir, yo

The SECRETARY OF THE TREASURY.

rMENT, *Revenue Office, January 27, 1794.*

niry into "the expediency of erecting a light-
ock inlet, and an estimate of the probable ex-
s.

Carolina, in time to have produced the infor-
e, in the session subsequent to that in which
t inspector, is represented as the cause of the
Edenton, who had been empowered to procure

the sea coast. *First*, that a small wooden light-
of North Carolina for the site of a light-house,
ive hundred dollars, per estimate A; and, *Se-*
cted upon the head land, or Cape of Hatteras,
ges and materials, would probably cost twenty

light-house, first mentioned, are, that it is the
he traders of the vicinity; that it will be useful
e night, and that it can be effected at the least
urns.

. The peculiarly dangerous nature of the navi-
uency and suddenness of gales and tempests.
to the several inlets of Pamplicoe and Albe-
to the numerous rich and increasing coasters,
atteras; and, lastly, to the numerous vessels
l on the American continent, to the southward
e Southern States.

fer at this time the erection of the light-house
t expedient to the State, were a comparison to
unds, Congress will, of course, have occasion
ly to the accommodation and security of the
th Carolina could not have been particularly

which either light-house would be erected, in
appears that both situations afford very good

ne part of the scene contemplated in the order
ly suggested in the two paragraphs of the pre-
patch in time of peace, and safety in time of
ly parts of our sea coast, as the vessels of the
hoals without sailing round them, when expe-
those courses. An intimate knowledge of the
vessels and those of small force from ships of

obedient servant,

H COXE, *Commissioner of the Revenue.*

Report of Commissioner of Revenue, Tench Coxe, January 27, 1794.

[1794. LIGHT-HOUSE ON THE COAS

3d CONGRESS.]

No. 20

LIGHT-HOUSE ON THE COAS

COMMUNICATED TO THE SENAT

The Secretary of the Treasury, pursuant to the order of the S
cretary of the Treasury to inquire into and report to Congr
light-house on Occracock island, or elsewhere, near the
probable expense," respectfully makes the following repor

Upon receipt of that order, he instructed the Commissione
care of that branch of the treasury business, which respects l
ries concerning the subject of it. But, having for a long time
of Cape Hatteras, would be an establishment of very general
it a fit occasion to unite with an examination of the scene indi
the Cape adapted to a light-house, and of such other circums
a judgment of the practicability and expediency of erecting
cordingly he charged the commissioner with the collateral inq
The result of the investigation on both points, is herewith
27th of January last, accompanied with an estimate of the ex
scene designated by the order.
It is submitted as the opinion of the Secretary, that it wou
first rate, on Cape Hatteras, (the requisite cession being previ
of the kind described in the estimate on the land ceded by th
All which is respectfull

ALEXA

TREASURY DEPARTMENT, *February* 20, 1794.

F NORTH CAROLINA. 265

[1st SESSION.

NORTH CAROLINA.

BRUARY 22, 1794.

of the 28th of March, 1792, "directing the Se-
their next session, the expediency of erecting a
ace of Occracock inlet, and an estimate of the

e revenue, (who is charged with the immediate
ouse establishments,) to make the proper inqui-
ained an opinion that a light-house on some part
to the navigation of the United States, he judged
by the order, an examination of the situations on
as were necessary to be attended to, in forming
aintaining a light-house on the Cape. And ac-
ikewise.
ted in a letter from the commissioner, dated the
of such an erection as appears eligible within the

advisable as well to erect a light-house, of the
btained for the purpose) as to establish a beacon
of North Carolina, for the site of a light-house.
itted.
. HAMILTON, *Secretary of the Treasury.*

Lighthouse on the Coast of North Carolina, communicated to the Senate, February 22, 1794.

266 COMMERCE AND NAVIGATION. [1794.

Estimate of the cost of building a lighted beacon, &c.

The building to be a wooden frame, fifty feet high, exclusively of the lanthorn. To contain one large lamp, with four wicks; to be twenty feet at the base, and to be reduced gradually to twelve feet at the top. It is thought necessary to continue the size of the building to that width at top, as it will be of great use as a sailing mark by day, and the larger the column the farther it may be visible.

Ranging timber, in board measure,	5,500 feet,
Scantling for framing in do.	2,500 feet,
Boards for floors and ceiling, &c.	2,800 feet,
Ditto for step ladders,	360 feet,
75 joists, board measure,	3,500 feet,
Waste of wooden materials,	1,000 feet,
	15,660 feet, at 16 dollars.

Including the charges of delivery at Occracock,		£93 19 2
Cedar to frame the windows and lanthorn,		10 00 0
Nails, spikes, bolts, locks, and hinges,		12 10 0
The lamp, and chains for it,		2 10 0
Glass for the lanthorn,		7 10 0
Ditto for the windows,		3 00 0
Workmanship, including the lanthorn, if of wood,		150 00 0
Painting three times,		20 00 0
If the lanthorn is made of iron and covered, &c. with copper, it would cost	£150	
Out of which might be deducted for one of wood,	40	
Leaves,		110 00 0
		£409 09 2
A house for the keeper, with a receptacle for oil, $400,		150 00 0
Total, $1,491 89, equal in Pennsylvania currency, to		£559 09 2

Estimate of the cost of building a lighted beacon, 1794.

SIR:
Having duly ex
Carolina, referred to y
has occurred thereon.
It does not appear
view to the shell ban
self to a comparison o
of sand banks, or isla
tion of the object of th
however, on account
no vessel could ventu
But, it has been sugge
rived at that place, to
It is found, on exa
ant in the course of th
tion, was communica
preferring the site on
is, however, reason to
erected on Shell Cast
It does not appear
if otherwise less cond
In a matter so per
lature of North Caro
mit of building on an
at Occracock island,
tion ever arose in the
The resolution of
situations; and it wa
Pamptico and Albe
causes. The report
who transmitted it:
Since the late ref
superintendent of th
the petitioners.
The minute and
to the mind, is not att
ted, on either Occrac
Carolina.
I have

The SECRETARY

Report of Commissioner of Revenue,
Tench Coxe, March 15, 1794.

A.

TREASURY DEPARTMENT, *Revenue Office, March 15th*, 1794.

the object of the petition of the merchants, masters of vessels, and pilots of North
e 20th instant by the House of Representatives, I have the honor to state to you what

report of the Inspector of the proposed site on Occracock island, that he extended his
ands which lie one or two miles within Pampticoe Sound; but that he confined him-
eral advantages which might be expected from light-houses, on some part of the chain
ich bound the ocean from Cape Hatteras to Cape Look-out. No immediate illustra-
n can, therefore, be obtained from the Inspector's report. It is worthy of observation,
t consideration suggested by the petitioners, that the Inspector has represented "that
e bar, or the swash, *in the night*, if there was a light-house erected near the inlet."
t a light on Shell Castle island, will be of use in enabling vessels, which shall have ar-
heir inward course to a more safe anchorage.
that the position desired by the petitioners, was contemplated by a principal inform-
directed by the Senate, and that a comparison of the two sites, now under considera-
im, favoring, in the first instance, the interior island, but, nevertheless, ultimately
k, because the island within was not then supposed to afford a safe foundation. There
that a lighted beacon, like that contemplated in the bill of the Senate, may be safely

e, that the greater facility of defence should incline to a preference of any position,
the proper uses of a light-house—*the warning* and *the direction* of navigators.
cal, it ought to be particularly remembered, that the original proceedings of the Legis-
ted out the position on Occracock island, without giving an extension which might ad-
nterior islands; and it appears, from the Inspector's report, that, during his examination
ted the pilots who reside on the spot, upon local points. Whether the present ques-
ences, is unknown at the treasury.
ate directing the inquiry, was in terms fully comprehending all the contemplated
nicated in September, 1792, to all the Collectors of the Customs, on the waters of
unds, in order to give due notoriety to a matter obviously liable to injury from local
spector was not made until June, 1793, and remains uncontradicted by the Collector,
y different result to their inquiries been transmitted by the other Collectors.
you, the ordinary use has been made of the nautical knowledge and experience of the
re establishments, and of his local knowledge. He does not coincide in opinion with

ocal knowledge requisite to the formation of a decided opinion, entirely satisfactory
It appears, however, indubitable, that a lighted beacon, of the limited value contempla-
d, or Shell Castle island, will be greatly beneficial to the trade and navigation of North

to be, with great respect, sir, your most obedient servant,

TENCH COXE, *Commissioner of the Revenue.*

TREASURY.

To the Honorable the Congress of the United States, the represen
masters of vessels and merchants, owners of vessels, tr

That they have understood there was a light-house about to be
have further understood, that a survey has been made of the harbo
as the place most proper to erect the light on. And as they have
erected for the benefit of vessels bound into or out of Occracoc
think the light-house should be erected on an island which stands
in preference of Occracock island.

1st. Because it will be a good mark for vessels to come in over
it will not, and can only serve to inform when opposite the bar.

2d. Because it will be a good mark for vessels to run roun
shoal, of a dark night, into safe anchorage, which would not be th
Royal shoal to Occracock is too great to trust to any bearing to go

3d. Because the materials for building the house can be cheape

4th. Because it will be a better mark to cross the Bluff shoal i
count of its being much nearer and more ahead. And they beg le
will not have a single advantage over that of the Castle, the found

5th. Because if, at any future period, it should be thought expe
Occracock, the place which we now recommend for the light-hous
fectually to protect the shipping.

3d CONGRESS.

LIGHT-HOUSE ON

COMMUNICATED TO

The Secretary of the Treasury, to whom

The paper A, herewith transmitted, (
the immediate superintendence of the ligh
been made in relation to the matter in qu

There has not hitherto been discover
tion, to that which was before contemplat
investigation have not been such as to a
expedite this report, as it is understood th
comparison of the two points.

TREASURY DEPARTMENT, *March 17th,*

Lighthouses on the Coast of North Carolina, communicated to the House of Representatives, March 17, 1794.

of the subscribers, pilots, of Occracock bar,
n and out at the same, showeth:

ontiguous to Occracock bar. And that they
report made in favor of Occracock island,
ason to believe the light is intended to be
beg leave to state the reasons why they
harbor of Occracock, called Shell Castle,

r, by night or by day, which, at Occracock,

uoy, atthe southwest point of the Royal
if at Occracock, as the distance from the
narrow a channel.
d at the Castle than any other place.
ight, than if it stood at Occracock, on ac-
her to add, that a light-house at Occracock
eing equally good.
erect a fort for the protection of vêssels at
e only spot where a fort can be erected ef-

CHARD WADE, *and fifty-six others.*

Petition of Pilots of Ocracoke Bar, masters of vessels, merchants, and owners of vessels, trading in and out of Ocracoke Inlet, for a lighthouse on Shell Castle Island rather than Ocracoke Island.

No. 21. [1st SESSION.

E COAST OF NORTH CAROLINA.

USE OF REPRESENTATIVES, MARCH 17, 1794.

erred the representation of Richard Wade and others, respectfully
s thereupon, as follows:
letter from the Commissioner of the revenue, who is charged with
establishments) exhibits the result of the investigation which has

ient ground for preferring the place advocated by the representa-
ely: the site on Occracock. But the opportunities for the future
a definitive judgment. It has, however been thought advisable to
from the Senate is pending before the House which may involve a

pectfully submitted.

ALEXANDER HAMILTON, *Secretary of the Treasury.*

298 COMMERCE AND NAVIGATION. [1794.

3d CONGRESS. No. 23. [1st SESSION.

LIGHT HOUSE ON THE COAST OF NORTH CAROLINA.

COMMUNICATED TO THE HOUSE OF REPRESENTATIVES, APRIL 15, 1794.

Mr. BLOUNT, from the committee to whom was referred a bill, sent from the Senate, entitled "An act to erect a Light House on the head land of Cape Hatteras, and a lighted Beacon on Ocracock Island, in the State of North Carolina," together with the representation of Richard Wade, and others, and the report of the Secretary of the Treasury thereon, reported:

That, for the reasons stated in the representation of Richard Wade, and others, which are said, by a gentleman who has been upwards of twenty years acquainted with the navigation of Ocracock Inlet, to be just, your committee are of opinion that the lighted Beacon proposed to be erected on Ocracock Island, ought to be erected on an Island in the harbor of Ocracock, called Shell Castle; but, as that Island is situate nearly a league within the bar, they think it would be proper to make the beacon five feet higher than has been proposed, and two feet broader at the base; and, therefore, they recommend the following amendments to the bill, viz:

Strike out, in the third and fourth lines of the second section, the words "certain land ceded to the United States by the State of North Carolina, aforesaid, situate on Ocracock Island, in said State," and insert, instead thereof, the words, "an island in the harbor of Ocracock, called Shel' Castle." Insert, in the fifth line of the second section, after the word "fifty," the word five; and, in the same line, after the word "twenty," the word two.

Lighthouses on the Coast of North Carolina, communicated to the House of Representatives, April 15, 1794.

CHAP. XXVIII.—*An Act to erect a Lighthouse on the headland of Cape Hatteras; and a lighted Beacon on Shell Castle Island in the harbor of Occacock in the state of North Carolina.*

SECTION 1. *Be it enacted by the Senate and House of Representatives of the United States of America in Congress assembled,* That as soon as the jurisdiction of so much of the head-land of Cape Hatteras in the state of North Carolina, as the President of the United States shall deem sufficient and most proper for the convenience and accommodation of a lighthouse shall have been ceded to the United States, it shall be the duty of the Secretary of the Treasury to provide by contract which shall be approved by the President of the United States, for building a lighthouse thereon of the first rate, and furnishing the same with all necessary supplies, and also to agree for the salaries or wages of the person or persons who may be appointed by the President for the superintendence and care of building said lighthouse: And the President is hereby authorized to make said appointments. That the number and disposition of the lights in the said lighthouse shall be such, as may tend to distinguish it from others, and as far as practicable, to prevent mistakes in navigators.

SEC. 2. *And be it further enacted,* That the Secretary of the Treasury be authorized to provide by contract, which shall be approved by the President of the United States, for building on an island in the harbor of Occacock, called Shell Castle, a lighted beacon of a wooden frame fifty-five feet high, to be twenty-two feet at the base, and to be reduced gradually to twelve feet at the top exclusively of the lantern, which shall be made to contain one large lamp with four wicks, and for furnishing the same with all necessary supplies. *Provided,* That no such lighted beacon shall be erected, until a cession of a sufficient quantity of land on the said island shall be made to the United States by the consent of the legislature of the state of North Carolina.

SEC. 3. *And be it further enacted,* That sufficient monies be appropriated for the erecting and completing the buildings aforesaid out of any monies heretofore appropriated which may remain unexpended, after satisfying the purposes for which they were appropriated, or out of any monies which may be in the treasury not subject to any prior appropriation.

APPROVED, May 13, 1794.

An Act to erect a Lighthouse on the headland of Cape Hatteras; and a lighted Beacon on Shell Castle Island in the harbor of Occacock in the state of North Carolina.

Appendix B[1]

OTHER LIGHTS AND LIGHTKEEPERS

Other lighthouses, light vessels, and beacon lights in the vicinity of Ocracoke in Pamlico Sound were:

Light Vessels	***Lighthouses***
Pamlico Point	North West Point of Royal Shoal
Ocracoke Channel	Long Shoal
Long Shoal	Beacon Island
Pamlico Point	Brant Island
Brant Island	Harbor Island
Nine Feet Shoal	

Lighthouses and light vessels were in isolated locations, making it hard to get needed supplies. Bids were taken from those wanting to acquire the job of transporting supplies to the light vessels and stations.

The following is an ad placed in the *Republican* (a newspaper published in Washington, N.C.) by the superintendent of lighthouses:

Superintendent's Office
District of Ocracoke
March 1st. 1839

1 PUBLISHER'S NOTE: This Appendix B was originally Chapter 6 in *Ocracoke Lighthouse.*

Proposals will be received at this office until the 31st. day of the present month for transportation of provisions, water, wood, oil, materials, and c.—for one year, from the 1st. April next, for 6 LIGHT-BOATS, stationed in Pamtico[2] Sound, viz:

LIGHT BOAT	at the mouth of Neuse River
" "	Brant Island Shoal
LIGHT BOAT	Harbour Island Bar
" "	S.W. Point of Royal Shoal
" "	Nine Feet Shoal
" "	Long Shoal

The articles required to be furnished will be delivered to Ocracoke or Portsmouth, at some store-house or landing, except the wood, which will be delivered to some landing in Neuse Bay or Pamtico[3] Sound—the transportation to be made quarterly, or oftener if required by the superintendent, payment to be made over after the expiration of each quarter.

S. Brown
Superintendent

Before the light vessels were constructed and placed into operation, the channels were marked and advertised in a local paper. One example of these notices is listed here:

Washington Gazette
Friday, July 24, 1807

Notice:
Of buoys placed in Pamlico Sound—by DAVID WALLACE JR. who was appointed to place buoys and give their bearings ... [bearings given] ... PORTSMOUTH, MAY 25, 1807

---

2 "Pamtico" was a common spelling for "Pamlico" in most records in the 1700s and early 1800s.

3 *ibid.*

Appendix B

SOME OF THE KEEPERS APPOINTED AT PAMLICO SOUND STATIONS AND VESSELS[4]

STATION	Keepers	Annual Salary	Appointed
BEACON ISLAND			
	J.T. Hunter	$350	Aug. 1855
	J. Orrow	350	Feb. 1850
PAMLICO POINT			
	Lemuel Fulford	400	May 1849
	William Brinn	400	March 1859
	Burton Shipp	400	
	N.W. Ireland	400	Sept. 1856
	Robert Wallace	400	Jan. 1867
	Stephen Fowler	500	July 1867
ROYAL SHOAL VESSEL			
	Anson Gaskill	500	May 1849
	Isaac W. Davis	500	Aug. 1850
	Anson Chadwick	500	May 1853
	George W. Styron	500	1854-1860
	Wallace Styron	500	Jan. 1869
NW POINT ROYAL SHOAL			
Keeper	Benj. Robinson	500	May 1857
1st asst.	L.J. Hunter	300	Jul. 1857
2nd asst.	Thomas Newby	300	Jul. 1857
1st asst.	Matilda Robinson	300	May 1859
Keeper	Benj. Lawrence	500	
Assist.	John W. Hill	300	
"	George Rose	300	
"	James Newbern	300	Feb. 1865
"	Thomas C. Jones	300	May 1865
"	J.J. McGourn	300	Dec. 1865
"	C.F. Austin	300	Apr. 1866

4 Microfilm, *Lighthouse Keepers*

STATION	*Keepers*	*Annual Salary*	*Appointed*
"	Edward B. Burns	300	Sept. 1866
Keeper	Thomas C. Jones	600	Sept. 1866
Assist.	George Smith	300	1866
"	George Mayo	300	Oct. 1866
"	Gedion Tolson	300	1867-68
"	Mary J. Jones	300	Jan. 1867
Keeper	Benj. Lawrence	600	1978
Asst.	Elija Dixon	440	1878
"	Charles B. Keeler	440	1878
"	James E. Harman	440	1878
Keeper	Benj. Lawrence	600	1879
Assist.	T.S. Gaskill	440	1879
"	E.S. Gaskill	440	1867-75
Keeper	L.C. Angill	600	1885-86
Assist.	Thos B. Spencer	440	1886-88
Keeper	E.L. Keeler	600	Jul. 1886
Assist.	Wallace Morris	440	Jun. 1886
"	F.M. Goodwin	440	1888-89
"	Joseph W. O'Neal	440	Mar. 1889
"	John W. O'Neal	440	1889-90
"	Alonzo English	440	1890-95
"	Susan D. Keeler	440	1895
HARBOR ISLAND			
Keeper	Gayer Chadwick	500	Jul. 1849
"	Oliver Chadwick	500	April. 1853
"	Gayer Chadwick	500	Feb. 1867
Asst.	Jeramiah Fidly	300	Feb. 1867
Keeper	W.B. Physive	600	Jul. 1867
Asst.	John Smith	400	Oct. 1867
"	Isaac Pender	400	Jan. 1869
Keeper	David Stanton	600	Jan. 1870
Asst.	Thomas C. Davis	440	1874-75
"	Thomas C. Davis	440	1875-79
Keeper	Wm T. Steward	600	1877-79
"	Martin F. Siar	600	1879

STATION	*Keepers*	*Annual Salary*	*Appointed*
"	John T. Shipp	600	1870
Asst.	Selden D. Delmar	440	1879
"	George W. Wade	440	1879
BRANT ISLAND			
Keeper	James Fountain	500	Feb. 1864
Asst.	W. Davis	300	1864
"	John Walktin	300	1864
"	John W. Hill	300	1864
Keeper	John W. Walkin	600	Mar. 1866
Asst.	Levi Rock	400	Jun. 1866
"	Thomas Wilkein	400	1866
"	John Canuly (?)	400	1866
"	Charles F. Price	400	1866
"	John F. Wilkins	400	1867
Keeper	Edward B. Hooper	600	1870
Assist.	Wade L. Harvey	400	1870
Keeper	George L. Smith	600	1872
Assist.	James D. Wilkin	400	1872
Keeper	Elijah L. Gaskill	600	1873
Asst.	J.C. Johnsont	400	1873
Keeper	Peter Johnston	600	1873
"	Charles B. Keeler	600	1833
Asst.	Edward S. Keeler	400	1877
"	Lazarus G. Hinnant	400	1886-87
Keeper	Wm. J. Simmons	600	1887-95
Asst.	Royal L. Ireland	400	1887-95
"	Chalcendany Lewis	400	1891-95
"	Lewis B. Austin	440	1894
"	Mrs. Lela Simmons	440	1895
Keeper	Lazarus Hinnant	600	1895-97
Asst.	Alonzo J. English	440	1895-1900
Keeper	Robert M. Jeannette	600	1897-1900
"	Alonzo J. English	600	1900
Asst.	W.L. Gaskill	440	1900

STATION	*Keepers*	*Annual Salary*	*Appointed*
LONG SHOAL LIGHT VESSEL			
Keeper	Christopher O'Neal	500	1849-appt to Shoal
"	Ronald Midgett	500	died Sept. 1853
"	Samuel Pugh	500	Mar. 1852
"	Robert Robinson	500	July. 1853
"	M.L. Shanberg	500	-
"	L.A. Wilson	500	1863
"	Ohn Best	500	1864
LONG SHOAL STATION			
Keeper	John Best	500	May 1867
Asst.	Wm. Hooper	400	Aug. 1867
Keeper	Nasa W. Farrow	600	Sept. 1867
Assist.	Wm. O'Neal	400	Oct. 1867
"	Sanderson Pain	400	Jan. 1869
"	Wm. P. O'Neal	400	1870-71
"	Francis P. Midgett	400	Jul. 1873
Keeper	Wm. H. Manley	600	1873-76
Asst.	Marcus L. Lewis	420	1873-76
Keeper	Elijah D. Dixon	600	1876-78
Asst.	Edward S. Keeler	420	1876-78
"	John J. Sharp	420	1878-79
"	John R. Pigott	420	1878
Keeper	Angus C. Thompson	600	1878
Assist.	John R. Pigott	420	1878

APPENDIX C

LETTERS CONCERNING THE TRANSFER OF OCRACOKE LIGHTHOUSE TO CAPE HATTERAS NATIONAL SEASHORE PARK

WALTER B. JONES
1st District, North Carolina

Telephone: Code 202: 225-3101

FLOYD J. LUPTON
Administrative Assistant

Committees
Agriculture
Merchant Marine
and Fisheries

Congress of the United States
House of Representatives
Washington, DC 20515

April 27, 1990

Ms. Ellen F. Cloud
Ocracoke, NC 27960

Dear Ellen:

May I take this opportunity to express to you my warm and sincere appreciation for the beautiful hand painted pictures of the Ocracoke Lighthouse constructed in 1823 and also for the replica of the Ocracoke Lighthouse.

These pictures mean so very much to me and especially the fact that you painted them enhances their value even more. We have a very special place in our home for the lighthouse, and we cordially invite you to visit with us in Belhaven whenever you are passing that way.

Over a period of time, it has been a real pleasure for me to assist you in all matters relating to the lighthouse, and I commend you on your dedicated efforts to maintain this structure in its original state. We will continue to remain active in this matter until such time as a generator has been installed, the lights taken from the guardrail and the windows are constructed and installed. Already a letter has been written to Admiral Yost, Commandant, US Coast Guard regarding the transfer of the Lighthouse structure from the Coast Guard to the National Park Service. I am informed that such a request was made about six months ago and is currently pending in the New York office of the Coast Guard. Please be assured of our continued interest in this or any other matter of mutual concern to you and the good citizens of Ocracoke and at such time as a response has been received from Admiral Yost regarding this transfer, you will be promptly advised.

With warm personal regards and best wishes, I am

Sincerely,

Floyd

Floyd J. Lupton
Administrative Assistant

FJL:Lbo

Letter to Ellen F. Cloud from Mr. Floyd J. Lutpon, administrative assistant to Congressman Walter B. Jones, April 27, 1990.

WALTER B. JONES

PHONE: CODE 202 225-3101

FLOYD J. LUPTON

Congress of the United States
House of Representatives
Washington, DC 20515

May 7, 1990

Ms. Ellen F. Cloud
Ocracoke, NC 27960

Dear Ellen:

During your recent visit to Washington, we discussed the Ocracoke Lighthouse and what appears to be the Coast Guard delay in the installation of the generator to supply power to the lighthouse and also the installation of the proper windows.

I have on this date discussed these two issues directly with Captain Parks, Director, Aids to Navigation 5th Coast Guard District in Portsmouth, VA. He later advised me that the generator system would be completely installed with appropriate wiring to the navigation light and the lights removed from the outside rail by the end of May 1990.

Regarding the windows, Captain Parks advised that the windows were being milled by the Williams Port Preservation Trading Center under the supervision of the National Park Service and would be completed and installed during the coming summer.

As of this date, we have not received a response to our letter directed to Admiral Paul Yost, Commandant, US Coast Guard, regarding the transfer of the lighthouse structure to the National Park Service. However, at such time as a response has been received, you will be promptly advised.

With warm personal regards and best wishes, I am

Sincerely,

Floyd J. Lupton
Administrative Assistant

FJL:Lbo

Letter to Ellen F. Cloud from Mr. Floyd J. Lutpon, administrative assistant to Congressman Walter B. Jones, May 7, 1990.

U.S. Department of Transportation

United States Coast Guard

Commandant
United States Coast Guard

Washington, DC
Staff Symbol: (G-CC/104)
Phone: (202) 366-4280

5730

MAY 10 1990

The Honorable Walter B. Jones
Chairman, Committee on Merchant Marine
and Fisheries
House of Representatives
Washington, DC 20515

Dear Mr. Chairman:

This is in response to your letter of April 27, 1990, regarding Ocracoke Island Lighthouse, and a proposal to transfer the structure to the National Park Service.

We support transferring historic light stations located on (or adjacent to) National Park properties to the National Park Service. The National Park Service has asked us, however, to undertake these transfers on a case by case basis. This allows the appropriate Park Service unit to properly plan and budget for the increased maintenance responsibility which they incur when they assume ownership of the properties. As you are aware, Cape Hatteras Lighthouse, which has an active Coast Guard light, is owned by the National Park Service.

Possible transfer of Ocracoke Lighthouse to the National Park Service has been discussed with Park Service staff at the Cape Hatteras National Seashore, but we have not yet received a formal request for this action. We intend to pursue the transfer, and believe the Park Service is the best agency to ensure continued protection of historic Ocracoke Light.

Sincerely,

CLYDE T. LUSK, JR.
Vice Admiral, U.S. Coast Guard
Acting Commandant

Letter to Congressman Walter B. Jones from the acting commandant of the U.S. Coast Guard, May 10, 1990.

WALTER B. JONES

FLOYD J. LUPTO

AGRICULTURE
MERCHANT MARINE AND FISHERIES

Congress of the United States
House of Representatives
Washington, DC 20515

May 16, 1990

Ms. Ellen F. Cloud
Ocracoke, NC 27960

Dear Ellen:

During your visit to Washington in late April, you discussed with Floyd the possible transfer of the Ocracoke Island Lighthouse structure to the National Park Service. Immediately following your visit, a request was made directly to Admiral Paul A. Yost, Jr., Commandant, US Coast Guard with a request that this action be taken.

I am attaching a copy of a letter received on this date from the Acting Commandant which is self-explanatory. Even though the Park Service has discussed the possible transfer of the Ocracoke Lighthouse from the Coast Guard to the Park Service, the Coast Guard has not yet received a formal request for this action. You will also note that the Coast Guard intends to pursue the transfer and believes that the National Park Service is the best agency to ensure continued protection of this historic structure. May I suggest that you discuss this matter with Mr. Thomas Hartman, Superintendent, Cape Hatteras National Seashore in an effort to ascertain whether or not an official request for transfer has been made as of this date.

Please be assured of my continued personal interest in this transfer or any other matter of mutual interest to you personally and to the good citizens of Ocracoke.

With warm personal regards and best wishes, I am

Sincerely,

Walt

WALTER B. JONES
Member of Congress

WBJ:boL
Attachment

Letter to Ellen F. Cloud from Congressman Walter B. Jones, May 16, 1990.

WALTER B. JONES

FLOYD J. LUPTO

AGRICULTURE

Congress of the United States
House of Representatives
Washington, DC 20515

May 16, 1990

Ms. Ellen F. Cloud
Ocracoke, NC 27960

Dear Ellen:

During your visit to Washington in late April, you discussed with Floyd the possible transfer of the Ocracoke Island Lighthouse structure to the National Park Service. Immediately following your visit, a request was made directly to Admiral Paul A. Yost, Jr., Commandant, US Coast Guard with a request that this action be taken.

I am attaching a copy of a letter received on this date from the Acting Commandant which is self-explanatory. Even though the Park Service has discussed the possible transfer of the Ocracoke Lighthouse from the Coast Guard to the Park Service, the Coast Guard has not yet received a formal request for this action. You vili also note that the Coast Guard intends to pursue the transfer and believes that the National Park Service is the best agency to ensure continued protection of this historic structure. May I suggest that you discuss this matter with Mr. Thomas Hartman, Superintendent, Cape Hatteras National Seashore in an effort to ascertain whether or not an official request for transfer has been made as of this date.

Please be assured of my continued personal interest in this transfer or any other matter of mutual interest to you personally and to the good citizens of Ocracoke.

With warm personal regards and best wishes, I am

Sincerely,

Walt

WALTER B. JONES
Member of Congress

WBJ:boL
Attachment

Letter to regional director, Southeast Region, United States Department of the Interior, from Mr. Thomas Hartman, superintendent, Cape Hatteras National Seashore, May 31, 1990.

Index[1]

Illustrations in italics

1 NOTE: Names listed on pages 82-84, 116, 133-43, 150, and 192-95 are not included in index unless otherwise mentioned in text.

The author on the porch of the Ocracoke Preservation Society museum, "my pride and joy," circa 1998.
AUTHOR COLLECTION

About the Author

ELLEN MARIE FULCHER CLOUD (1940-2016) was a prolific Outer Banks historian and genealogist, channeling her interest in Ocracoke and Portsmouth islands into at least a dozen works, including three books. An Ocracoke native who traced her lineage to the earliest settlers, Ellen aided many with her research and personally helped countless descendants research their own families.

Ellen grew up on remote Ocracoke, living there until 1963 and returning in 1983. Her early passions included dancing and listening to the rock and roll of North Carolina's Outer Banks. She became a self-taught historian, focusing on Ocracoke and Portsmouth, and engaged in sea-related sketchwork, some of which found its way into her books. She also was a preservationist and community leader, helping retrieve the original windows for a restoration of the Ocracoke lighthouse. In 1996, she moved to the mainland but remained close to "the Banks."

In addition to *Ocracoke Lighthouse* and *Old Salt*, Ellen authored *Portsmouth: The Way It Was* as part of her "Island History" trilogy. She was active with the Ocracoke Preservation Society, Friends of Portsmouth Island, and, in later years, the local history study group in Atlantic and Harkers Island, North Carolina. In addition to her work, she left her wish: "I want people to remember me with laughter."

Books That Endure
BEACH GLASS
BOOKS
BeachGlassBooks.com